WORLD WAR I
ON LAND

Peter Hepplewhite is an escaped history teacher, currently hiding in the Tyne and Wear Archives Service, where he works as Education Officer. He has been a freelance writer for more than ten years, starting with school textbooks (boo!) before he realized that war stories were more thrilling.

Although David Wyatt is primarily known for his work on fiction, including novels by Terry Pratchett and Philip Pullman, he has a love of history and enjoys the education he receives when working on factual projects. He lives on Dartmoor, which is stuffed full of history, as well as amazing landscapes to stimulate his overactive imagination.

WORLD WAR I
ON LAND

PETER HEPPLEWHITE

Illustrations and maps by David Wyatt

MACMILLAN CHILDREN'S BOOKS

First published 2003 by Macmillan Children's Books
a division of Macmillan Publishers Limited
20 New Wharf Road, London N1 9RR
Basingstoke and Oxford
www.panmacmillan.com

Associated companies throughout the world

ISBN 0 330 41010 5

1 3 5 7 9 8 6 4 2

A CIP catalogue record for this book is available from
the British Library.

Typeset by Nigel Hazle
Printed and bound in Great Britain by Mackays of Chatham plc, Kent

To John Bonallie, for many happy years of jokes and anecdotes. And no, John, I'm not paying you for all those 'useful facts'!

CONTENTS

'THE GREAT WAR'

In August 1914 the showdown between the great powers of Europe began. The Allies – Britain, France and Russia – lined up against the Central Powers: Germany and Austria-Hungary. By the end of the year Europeans were already calling this 'the Great War'. No one expected the fighting to be so ferocious and no one could find a way to win. New and terrible weapons, especially artillery, machine guns, aeroplanes and barbed wire, brought a bloody stalemate and the deaths of millions. The killing lasted for four long years.

Alliance Trip Wire 1914

In 1914 most countries in Europe were bound together in tight alliances – so when the fighting began everyone piled in, like a deadly playground scrap. The crisis was triggered by the assassination of Archduke Franz Ferdinand in Sarajevo, Serbia, on 28 June.

- **Thwack!** Franz Ferdinand was the heir to the Austro-Hungarian throne. His death led an outraged Austria-Hungary to declare war on Serbia.
- **Thwack!** Russia, the ally of Serbia, began to **mobilize** a vast army on the Austro-Hungarian and German borders.
- **Thwack!** To hit first, Austria-Hungary's ally, Germany, declared war on Russia and Russia's main partner, France.
- **Thwack!** To knock out France, Germany launched the Schlieffen Plan – a huge attack through neutral Belgium.
- **Thwack!** Britain was dragged into the war to protect Belgium. The British Expeditionary Force (BEF) of 100,000 men left for France.

Hopes of a short, sharp fight were soon dashed as the opposing armies dug in on the Western Front – over 400 miles (600 km) of trenches stretching from the Swiss border to the English Channel. Troops from all over the British Empire – India, Canada, New Zealand and Australia – flocked to Britain's aid, while Algerians and Africans fought alongside the French. Turkey joined the Central Powers.

1915

The Germans tried to break through British lines in Belgium and were the first to use poisonous gas. Stalemate on the Western Front led the Allies to attack Turkey at Gallipoli and Mesopotamia (Iraq). The passenger liner *Lusitania* was sunk by a German **U-boat** off the Irish coast, sparking rage in the USA, because many American civilians drowned. The bloodshed was carried across the Alps when Italy joined the Allies. London suffered its first Zeppelin raid, and aircraft on the Western Front were armed with machine guns – the war had spread to the air. Sir Douglas Haig became commander of the BEF.

1916

By January 1916 2.5 million volunteers had joined the British army, but this was not enough. Conscription was introduced. Germany launched a huge attack against the French at Verdun. In the war at sea, the Royal Navy faced its sternest test since Trafalgar, over a century before: the Battle of Jutland. The result was a draw, but the German High Seas fleet feared another showdown and stayed in port after this. On 1 July 20,000 British soldiers were killed on the first day of the Battle of the Somme, and the fighting there went on until November. Lloyd George took over from Herbert Asquith as British Prime Minister. Hindenburg became the German Chief of Staff.

1917

German U-boats almost cut off British food supplies from North America. The USA entered the war in April, and in November the communists seized power in Russia and sought peace terms from Germany. The British tried to break through enemy lines at Passchendaele with a huge loss of life.

1918

In March Germany launched a massive spring offensive and drove a wedge between the British and French armies. Haig issued his famous 'backs to the wall' order: 'Every position must be held to the last man.' By the end of April this attack was exhausted and the tide slowly turned in favour of the Allies. The last 100 days of the war began on 8 August with a great Allied victory at the Battle of Amiens. The Germans called this 'the Black Day' because they lost 27,000 men in casualties and prisoners. In the weeks that followed British and Empire troops drove the enemy relentlessly back. On 9 November **Kaiser** Wilhelm abdicated. At 11:00 on 11 November the war ended. Cheering crowds danced in the streets of London and Paris.

1919

The Paris Peace Conference led to the Treaty of Versailles. In it, Germany was blamed for the war, lost territory and paid huge compensation to the Allies.

Britain survived but at a heavy cost: 700,000 dead and debts of £1,000 million to the USA (about £1,250 billion today). Paying the interest on this debt took half the nation's taxes during the 1920s and 1930s.

War Stories
This book highlights six stunning stories from this gruelling war and gives you the fighting facts behind them.

• *The Christmas Truce*
Christmas 1914. Life in the trenches is miserable – cold, wet and extremely dangerous. But then there is hope, in the form of an unofficial ceasefire. But what will the generals say? Bruce Bairnsfather is in the front line on one of the strangest days of the war.

• *An Underground War*
Mysterious explosions rock the British line from December 1914 – the Germans are using mines. Something must be done, and quickly, but can the 'clay-kickers' (tunnellers) save the day?

• *Gallipoli – a Side Show*
With the war dragging on in Europe, the Allies are looking for a quick fix. Will an attack against Turkey solve all their problems?

• *Guests of the Kaiser*

The Canadian Baron Richardson Racey is captured during a German gas attack. Can he escape the grim camps and reach the safety of neutral Holland?

• *The Prisoners' Martyr – Edith Cavell*

In 1915 Edith Cavell is running an escape network for Allied prisoners in Belgium. Why is the prim and proper daughter of a Norfolk vicar taking such a risk . . . and why does she freely admit her actions to the enemy?

• *Aftermath*

Who is the Unknown Warrior and why is he so important?

If your reading ends up in no man's land, help is at hand. Words shown in **bold** type are explained in Trench Talk or the Glossary on pages 127–30.

Never Mind

If the sergeant drinks your rum, never mind
And your face may lose its smile, never mind
He's entitled to a tot but not the bleeding lot
If the sergeant drinks your rum, never mind.

When old Jerry shells your trench, never mind
And your face may lose its smile, never mind
Though the sandbags burst and fly, you have
    only once to die,
When old Jerry shells your trench, never mind.

If you get stuck on the wire, never mind
And your face may lose its smile, never mind
Though you're stuck there all the day, they
    count you dead and stop your pay
If you get stuck on the wire, never mind.

Trench song

THE CHRISTMAS TRUCE

BATTLE BRIEFING

The Western Front

When World War I broke out in August 1914 the news was greeted by cheering crowds and yells of 'On to Berlin' or 'On to St Petersburg'. Most people believed there would be a decisive battle like Waterloo, a century before, and the troops would be home by Christmas. It wasn't to be.

German hopes lay in the Schlieffen Plan – a mighty right hook through Belgium to get behind the main French army and take Paris. It almost worked. The BEF and the French Fifth Army were hurled back, until a last desperate stand was made on the River Marne. This in turn forced the Germans to retreat and both sides began the so-called 'race to the sea' – fierce and bloody attempts to **outflank** each other and capture the Channel ports.

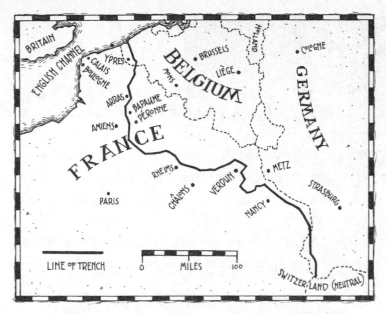

The Western Front, 1914

By November this war of movement was over and opposing trench systems had been dug from the Channel to Switzerland. Early attempts to punch a way through ended in terrible slaughter, as tens of thousands of men fell amid the chatter of machine guns. The pattern of the war was set for the next three and a half years: mud, blood, death and misery.

During the bleak winter of 1914–15 the BEF held the line in Belgium. Among the unlucky soldiers was Bruce Bairnsfather, a machine-gun officer in the Royal Warwickshire Regiment. He had just arrived, fresh and optimistic, from England and was about to get his first taste of trench warfare ... and a very unexpected Christmas.

9

SILENT NIGHT

Trench Life

Bruce never forgot his first spell in the trenches – few soldiers did. To escape the storm of German guns, his battalion moved up after dusk to a turnip field next to the huge Bois (forest) de Ploegsteert. The British **Tommies** had soon shortened this elegant Belgian name to 'Plugstreet Wood'.

The Plugstreet trenches zigzagged across the field and offered only poor protection against enemy fire. These

Bruce Bairnsfather

A British trench at Messines Ridge, considerably dried and better organized than those experienced by Bruce in 1914

were the 'Mark 1 trenches', little more than shallow ditches hastily cut into the clay. They had few of the later luxuries of frontline life, such as corrugated-iron sheets for roofing, wooden duckboards to walk on or sandbag supports for the oozing walls. British generals were still sure that they would break through the German lines early in 1915, so what was the point of wasting effort on trenches that would soon be left far behind?

It had been raining dismally for days and the ground was saturated as the Warwickshires sloshed in. Bruce saw to it that his machine guns were set up and gunners settled for the night. This was not easy, since the rain had washed away many of the **dugouts** left by earlier units and they had to be carved out of the slithery mud again. Now it was time for him to try to snatch a damp sleep, but where? Together with his sergeant, Bruce made two shallow caves from the soaking clay, one behind the other, and crawled in. As he lay down on his wet coat, he thought dismally about his first night in the trenches:

> Here I was in this horrible clay cavity, somewhere in Belgium, miles and miles from home, cold, wet through and covered with mud. Nothing could be heard except the occasional crack of the sniper's shot. In the narrow space beside me lay my equipment: my revolver and a sodden packet of cigarettes. Everything was cold, dark and damp. As far as I could see the future contained nothing but the same thing or worse ...

Bruce couldn't have known how right he was. After a short, uncomfortable doze he was woken by shouts and struck his head on the dugout ceiling as he sat up.

'We're bein' flooded out, sir,' the sergeant yelled. 'The water's a foot deep!'

As Bruce looked round, he realized he had been lying in a deepening pool and his clothes were soaked. The rest of the night was spent bailing out and vainly trying to dam the flood. The dismal work was lit by the menacing glare of German **star shells**.

Billets
Trench life, like the first glutinous night spent by Bruce,

was so hard and dismal that troops soon became exhausted. Another officer in Belgium, Major Bonham-Carter, wrote:

The continual standing on wet ground, the wearing of wet boots for several days without a change and of wet clothes have a very bad effect on the men, who in some cases can barely move when they leave the trenches.

To keep soldiers fighting fit, a tour of duty in the front lines was rewarded with a few days in support lines – 'in rest'. They would leave grey with weariness and caked in dirt, but with every step towards **billets** and a break their mood improved. Unbroken sleep, a hot bath, clean clothes and a decent meal did wonders for soldiers' spirits. Wages, a bob a day (5p) for an ordinary infantryman, were paid on the first day out of line. The money was soon spent, however, on cigarettes, women and cheap white wine.

Bruce remembered other simpler pleasures too: 'One could walk about the fields nearby, could read, write letters and sleep as much as one liked.' You can guess then that he was not exactly delighted to hear that his battalion was due back in the Plugstreet trenches for Christmas. 'So that's the festivities knocked on the head,' he moaned. What he could not have known was that Christmas 1914 was to be one of the strangest days of the war.

Christmas Eve

As the Warwickshires 'went in' again on 23 December, a small miracle improved their mood – it stopped raining. The weather became fine and cold. When Bruce woke on the morning of Christmas Eve he looked out on a scene that was almost beautiful. The frozen swamp of mud between the lines glistened with frost in the sun. There was even a fine sprinkling of snow in places.

The spirit of peace seemed to infect both armies. There was no shelling and little rifle fire. Plans were made for parties in the British dugouts and Bruce spent the evening at a special trench dinner for officers – there was a bottle of red wine and 'a medley of tinned things from home' to go with the usual **bully beef**. About 22:00 he was back in his own dugout when the sound of a German band and singing drifted over.

'Do you hear the **Boches** kicking up that racket over there?' Bruce quipped to his platoon commander.

'Yes, they've been at it some time.'

'Come on, let's go along the trench to the hedge there on the right – that's the nearest point to them, over there.'

As the two men moved closer they could hear the band scratching out a version of '**Deutschland, Deutschland über Alles**'. British 'mouth organ experts' hit back with ragtime songs and a copy of the German tune.

Suddenly Bruce heard a shout, 'Come over here', in a strong German accent.

This was met by rude blasts from mouth organs and mocking laughter. Then, after a short lull, a British sergeant yelled, 'Come over here.'

'You come halfway, I come halfway,' the German replied.

'Come on then!' shouted the sergeant. 'I'm coming along the hedge.'

'Ah, but there are two of you.'

At last one wary British sergeant and one cautious German moved slowly and suspiciously towards each other. Both had the same fears.

Was it a trap?

Could the Tommy/**Hun** be trusted to come alone?

In sight now.

Careful. Watch him.

Only a few yards.

They met.

As Bruce and the other Warwickshires listened, they could hear a smattering of conversation taking place out there in the darkness. Then the sergeant came back. He gleefully showed off the cigars and cigarettes he'd swapped for a tin of Capstan tobacco. He was safe. Bruce recalled: 'It had given just the requisite touch to our Christmas Eve, something a little human and out of the ordinary routine.' But there was more to come.

Christmas Day
Most people have a fantasy Christmas present in mind.

When he stirred on Christmas morning Bruce imagined a big one:

I should like to have suddenly heard an immense siren blowing; everybody to stop and say, 'What was that?' Siren blowing again; appearance of a small figure running across the frozen mud waving something. He gets closer – a telegraph boy with a wire! He hands it to me. With trembling fingers I open it: 'War off, return home – George R.I.' [the King]

The reality wasn't too bad though. The morning was fine and crisp. The cratered turnip field looked its best ... and the Germans were up to something! As he looked out of his trench, Bruce saw a lot of unusual activity:

*Heads were bobbing about and showing over their parapet in a most reckless way ... A complete Boche figure suddenly appeared and looked about itself. This complaint became infectious. It didn't take 'Our Bert' long to be up on the skyline (it is one long grind to ever keep him off it). This was the signal for more Boche anatomy to be disclosed and this was replied to by all our Alfs and Bills until, in less time than it takes to tell, half a dozen or so each of the **belligerents** were outside their trenches and advancing towards each other in no man's land. A strange sight, truly.*

After a minute Bruce joined his wayward men. Dressed in a muddy khaki suit, a green sheepskin coat and a balaclava helmet, he sauntered towards German lines. It was so confusing, especially for an officer of the British Army. Here were the enemy they were all supposed to hate, capering about in the open. He couldn't help his nit-picking first impressions:

> *The difference in type between our men and theirs was very marked. Our men in their costumes of dirty khaki with headdresses of woollen hats and mufflers were light-hearted, open and humorous as opposed to the sombre demeanour and stolid appearance of the Huns in their grey-green faded uniforms, top boots and pork-pie hats.*

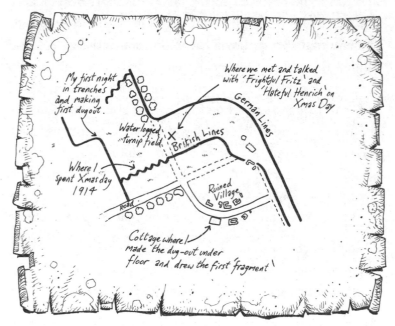

Map of the truce

Yet as the troops mingled in the middle of the turnip field, Bruce's feelings changed. **Fritz** was human too. Curious German soldiers inspected him and asked, '*Offizier?*' He nodded in reply. Everyone started to talk, smile . . . and laugh. There was fervent souvenir hunting.

Bruce chatted to a German lieutenant and, 'being a bit of a collector', pointed to their buttons.

> *We both said things to each other which neither*
> *understood, and agreed to a swap. I brought out my*
> *wire clippers and with a few deft snips removed a*
> *couple of his buttons and put them in my pocket. I*
> *then gave him two of mine in exchange.*

Meanwhile, the gathering was becoming more relaxed and comfortable. One of the Germans ran to his trench and came back with a large camera. The soldiers, Bruce included, posed together for several shots. He couldn't help but wonder if one day they would end up on a German mantelpiece while an old soldier bragged of the occasion a group of perfidious English surrendered unconditionally on Christmas Day.

After about an hour the party began to break up on the friendliest of terms. And, as he strolled back, Bruce was left with a lingering image:

> *One of my machine gunners, who was a bit of an*
> *amateur hairdresser in civil life, was cutting the*
> *unnaturally long hair of a docile Boche, who was*

patiently kneeling on the ground whilst the automatic
clippers crept up the back of his neck.

The Christmas mood lingered for a while. The Warwickshires stayed in the lines for another two days and there was no fighting. Bruce was able to indulge his collecting habit again too. He'd had his eye on a German rifle that had been lying near a couple of corpses for almost a month. Any earlier attempt to bag it would have been fatal, but now he simply walked over, picked it up and returned without any trouble. For his men, there was more singing and the treat of night-time fires without the risk of a sniper's bullet.

But the generals on both sides were furious as news of the Christmas truce spread. What on earth was going on? And how dangerous was it? Would the men start to disobey orders too?

The Warwickshires and other unwarlike units on both sides were ordered out of the line. For their replacements it was business as usual.

FIGHTING FACTS

A Cartoon War
In January 1915 life on the front line looked up for Bruce. He and a squad of men were detailed to defend

the ruined village of St Yvon. Among the battered houses there was one that was a little less damaged by shellfire. This was to become his 'home' for two months. Mercifully, it was dry and free from mud, but with a roof came other problems. No one dared to move during the day in case the sharp-eyed Germans realized that the ruins were occupied and

"Well, If you knows of a better 'ole, Go to it."

Bruce Bairnsfather became one of the most popular cartoonists of the war among the troops, because he conveyed their point of view

started pounding the village again. Faced with hours of enforced idleness, he took up an old hobby and began to draw cartoons.

Bruce sketched on scraps of paper, wooden ration boxes, the crumbling plaster walls of the cottage – in fact, on any clean, dry surface. His subjects were the men around him and the miserable surroundings they lived in, but were always drawn with humour and a joke. His work became so popular that visitors helped themselves to favourite scenes and took them to decorate their grimy dugouts. Encouraged by this, he sent his first cartoon, 'Where did that one go to?' to the *Bystander* magazine. It was accepted and his career as a cartoonist began.

The Trench Experience

In 2002 the BBC showed a TV programme called *The Trench*. A group of modern volunteers re-created the

British troops leave the safety of their trench to go 'over the top'

lives of World War I soldiers, living in the open – whatever the weather.

Bruce would have been fascinated. He had already thought of the idea and in 1916 wrote his own 'tongue in cheek' instructions for anyone in England curious enough to want to share the 'trench experience':

> I recommend the following procedure. Select a flat ten-acre ploughed field, so sited that all the surface water of the surrounding country drains into it. Now cut a zigzag slot four feet deep and three wide diagonally across, dam off as much water as you can so as to leave about 100 yards of squelchy mud, delve out a hole at one side of the slot then try to live there for a month on bully beef and biscuits, whilst a friend has instructions to fire at you with his Winchester (rifle) every time you put your head above the surface.

Football Fun

Many British and German troops were ardent football fans and there are several reports that ordinary soldiers carried footballs in their knapsacks, always eager for a 'kickabout'. Captain J. L. Jack of the Scottish Rifles wrote of his own men: 'However tired the rascals may be for parades, they always have enough energy for football.'

It was hardly surprising, then, that organizing a game against the enemy soon sprang to mind during the Christmas Truce. Of course, there were problems. In many areas no man's land was a muddy, pulverized and frozen mess. Nevertheless, plans were made.

Private William Trapp of the Warwickshires, based near Plugstreet Wood, noted: 'We are trying to arrange a football match with them [a German unit from Saxony] for tomorrow, Boxing Day.' To his annoyance British artillery fire put an end to the scheme. But others were more successful. One of the best stories was told by an old soldier, Ernie Williams, in a TV interview in 1983. He was serving in the 6th Cheshires near Wulverghem in Belgium:

The ball appeared from somewhere, I don't know where, but it came from their side. They made up some goals and one fellow went in goal and then it was just a general kickabout. I should think there were about a couple of hundred taking part. I had a go at the ball. I was pretty good then, at nineteen. Everybody seemed to be enjoying themselves. There was no referee and no score, no tally at all ...Those great big boots [army boots] we had on were a menace – and in those days the balls were made of leather and they soon got very soggy.

Christmas Treats

Every British soldier, and the 1,500 nurses serving alongside them, was sent a Christmas present in the name of King George V's daughter, 17-year-old Princess Mary. The small brass box held cigarettes, a pipe and pipe tobacco, a photograph of the Princess and a Christmas card greeting in the King's handwriting: 'May God protect you and bring you home safe.' For non-smokers there was a tin of sweets and some writing paper and for nurses, chocolates and a card. Over 400,000 royal presents were shipped out and delivered by 25 December. There were so many that complaints were received because they were filling up the supply trains to the front – and ammunition was being left behind!

Truce Tales

The Christmas Truce didn't stop fighting along the whole of the Western Front, but troops in many areas did cease fire for a while. And there were reports of heart-warming incidents on all sides.

Carol Competition

Graham Williams of the London Rifle Brigade remembered an unusual carol concert:

> They finished their carol so we thought we ought to retaliate, so we sang 'The First Noel', and when we finished that they all began clapping: and they struck up another favourite of theirs, 'O Tannenbaum'. And so it went on ... when we started 'O Come, All Ye Faithful' the Germans immediately joined in, singing the same hymn to the words 'Adeste, Fideles'. And I thought this is a really extraordinary thing – two nations singing the same carol in the middle of a war.

Operatic War

The German Crown Prince Wilhelm, son of the Kaiser, decided to visit his troops on Christmas Eve. He was Commander of the German Fifth Army, stationed in the Argonne region of France. As he moved forward there was the usual grim face of war: the howl of shells, bursts of machine-gun fire and the crump of trench mortars. Yet Wilhelm recalled, 'Every dugout had its Christmas tree, and from all directions came the sound of rough men's voices singing our exquisite old songs.'

And if it was songs the soldiers wanted, they were in for a wonderful surprise. The Prince had brought a star from the Berlin Opera with him, Walter Kirchoff, the tenor. While Wilhelm handed out Iron Crosses (medals) in the safety of the reserve trenches, Kirchoff went up to the front line to perform. The next day he told the Prince that 'some French soldiers had climbed up on to the **parapet** to applaud, until at last he gave them an encore'.

Just Like Diwali

Thousands of Indian troops served alongside the British and saw heavy fighting. The Garhwal Rifles, dug in near the village of Neuve-Chapel, were having a miserable time. Their trenches were a little downhill from those of the enemy and when the Germans pumped the water from their lines it flowed straight into those of the unlucky Garhwalis.

But on Christmas Eve the normally fierce Germans began behaving strangely. The Indians could hear them singing carols and watched in astonishment as they placed small candle-lit trees in rows along their parapets. The candles struck a chord with the Garhwalis. During the Hindu festival of Diwali, celebrated each autumn, earthenware oil lamps are lit in the evening and set up in rows outside temples and houses. In the middle of a European winter it was a reminder of home.

Wotcha, Cock. How's London?

Graham Williams of the London Rifles enjoyed the truce more than most. He was a fluent German speaker and in great demand on Christmas morning. He was having a good chinwag with a group of Germans in no man's land when one piped up in a broad cockney accent, 'Wotcha, Cock. How's London?'

Taken aback, Graham replied, 'Good Lord, you speak like a Londoner.'

German: 'Well, I am a Londoner!'

Graham: 'Well, what on earth are you doing in the German army?'

German: 'I'm a German – a German Londoner.'

Graham recalled:

Apparently he had been born in Germany, but had gone to London as a baby with his parents, who had a small business in the East End somewhere. He'd been brought up in England and gone to school in England. But by German law he was still a German national – he'd never been naturalized [become a British citizen] – he had been called up to Germany to do his national service: they did three years at that time. And afterwards he came back to London, joined his parents and got a job as a porter at Victoria station.

Old Joe Whip

Sing to the tune of the chorus of 'Casey Jones'

Old Joe Whip, mounted on the parapet
Old Joe Whip, a **Mills bomb** in his hand,
Old Joe Whip, he stopped a blooming **whizzbang**
Now he's a bomber in the promised land.

Trench song

AN UNDERGROUND WAR

BATTLE BRIEFING

The Ypres Salient

During the autumn of 1914 the British army held little more than 20 miles (32 km) of trenches on the Western Front. The key to this sector was the ancient cloth-making town of Ypres and the ground held in front of it – the grim Ypres **salient**. This formed a bulge in the British line that stuck out for 3 miles (5 km), like a crooked nose on a face (see map). And like a nose, it was just as vulnerable in a fight.

Still hopeful of a quick victory, the Germans launched a ferocious attack to break through to the sea on 20 October – the first Battle of Ypres. The British were outnumbered two to one in men and five to one in artillery, but managed to hang on. On one appalling day, the astonished Tommies watched as thousands of soldiers in long grey lines advanced towards

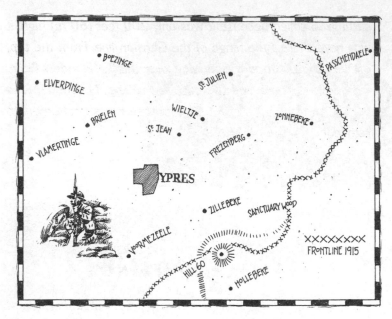

Map of the area surrounding Ypres

them, arms locked together and singing. They were student volunteers, thrown into battle with only six weeks' training. British artillery and machine guns ripped the lines to pieces. In three weeks 36,000 students died, a loss the Germans still call the Kindermord – the Massacre of the Children.

Although beaten back, the Germans made some key gains during November. They dug in on the Messines Ridge, a 15-mile (24-km) spine of higher ground that partly encircled Ypres. And, crucially, they captured the highest point of the ridge – Hill 60.

Yet to call it a hill was an absurdity. Hill 60 was a man-made mound, built with the spoil from a nearby railway cutting. So called because it was only 200 feet (60 m) high, it was nevertheless the hinge of the German line. From the top, artillery spotters had a clear view over the flat Flanders Plain, especially of Ypres and the exposed salient. No sooner had the German attacks stopped than the British schemed to retake it.

Panoramic view of Hill 60, near Ypres, 10 April 1915

Infantry assaults soon became fruitless slaughters and early in 1915 the generals realized it was time to try something different. Something the Germans had already used with stunning results – mining. Now it was time to strike back ... and the target was Hill 60.

TUNNELLING TERRORS

Indian Nightmare

Indian troops had been holding 10 miles (16 km) of the British line, near Festubert, since November 1914. But they were uneasy. Many were worn out by hard fighting and the miserable weather of a European winter. And then there were the rumours. Some men swore they had heard muffled banging, others the cushioned sound of digging. A few had been told that pilots in the Royal Flying Corps had seen mounds of discoloured soil behind enemy lines. Could it be that the Germans were digging mines under their feet? Or was this simply more idle trench gossip?

On 19 December torrential rain fell endlessly and there was no time for tittle-tattle. Trenches flooded, **fire steps** were washed away and, despite the soldiers' best efforts, their rifles often clogged with mud and jammed. At dawn on 20 December heavy German artillery and mortar fire seared the whole of the sector. Enemy attacks punched in near Givenchy and were hurled back only after bitter **skirmishes**.

Then, at 09:00, three mysterious flares arced into the air over the German trenches. Moments later 10 terrific explosions rocked the line held by the Sirhind Brigade. The ground shook and split. Tons of earth, together with men and weapons, were tossed 20 feet (6 m) in the air. The rumours were true. The Germans had tunnelled under the Indian trenches and fired powerful mines. Everyone close by was killed, while anyone within 160 feet (50 m) was knocked out or too dazed to fight on.

Waves of German assault troops dashed across no man's land and stormed the Indian lines. In the dugouts they found the bodies of dozens of men sitting as if they were asleep – killed by the explosions. Reinforcements were rushed in, but it was not until 22 December that the enemy was driven off. The first underground attack of the war had been stunningly successful.

Clay-kickers

In England one man was already working hard to hit back. Norton Griffiths was the Member of Parliament for Wednesbury in the West Midlands and the wealthy owner of a contracting business. He had made his fortune building railways and running mining operations around the world. A larger-than-life character, he was tall, handsome and outrageously confident. No sooner had the fighting begun than he turned his immense energy to helping the war effort. And he reckoned he had just the idea the army needed: clay-kicking!

In Britain Griffiths and Company had won the contract to build the Manchester sewerage system. Miles of underground tunnels were being driven through the clay subsoil by a group of elite miners using an unusual technique. They sat with their backs supported by a wooden framework and kicked their spades into the clay. The spoil was then passed back to a mate for removal. Proudly, the Manchester workers nicknamed themselves 'Moles' and their method 'clay-kicking'. In the right conditions they were the best miners in the world. Just the men needed, thought Norton, for digging tunnels under the enemy's trenches.

For weeks he badgered the War Office with a scheme

to take a force of Moles to France, but his pleas were ignored until the success of German mining operations. By February 1915 the enemy had exploded more mines and British troops had come to dread these underground explosions more than machine-gun fire or the crash of shells. Protests poured in from frontline officers. Something must be done, they demanded, or morale would collapse.

At last, on 14 February, Norton was summoned to see Field Marshal Kitchener, the Secretary of State for War, and given a chance to explain his ideas. In a dramatic pantomime, he snatched the coal shovel from the fireplace, sat on the floor and clay-kicked for his one-man audience. Kitchener was entranced and ordered him to go to France to consult with the top officers in the Royal Engineers (the army's own force of builders and engineers). This time, Norton found himself banging on an open door. The Royal Engineers welcomed his input and agreed there was an urgent need for expert mining units. By 19 February the War Office agreed to form the first eight tunnelling companies as soon as possible.

Norton flung his energy into finding recruits. Among the first were 18 of his Manchester clay-kickers. Before long, they were joined by miners of every type from across the country, including Scottish coal miners, Welsh slate miners and Cornish tin miners. And an unattractive lot they looked to army eyes – many were unusually small, others middle-aged and more than a few in their sixties, with white hair and missing teeth. They didn't take kindly to army discipline and were known to argue openly with their officers. One compensation was the pay – 6s 6d a day (32.5p), far higher than ordinary soldiers earned and better than most were paid in their civilian jobs. Norton added his own exciting spin to those he met personally: 'When the plunger's pressed, boys,' he said, grinning, 'you'll have a front-seat view of the Germans going up.'

Other men with mining experience were already in the army. They had joined up when the war began and now the call went out for them to transfer to the tunnelling companies.

One volunteer was Private Garfield Morgan of the South Wales Borderers. His career began with a rebellion. Twelve ex-miners from the Borderers were sent to London to be interviewed by Norton. On the way they were given a warning by the friendly sergeant-major who escorted them: 'Watch out. He might try to sign you up for 2s 2d [12.5p]. That's standard **sapper** pay. Stick out for the higher rate.'

One by one they filed in to see Norton, were offered 2s 2d and, to his fury, turned it down.

'Get out!' he yelled to each.

Forlornly, they prepared to march away when a booming voice called out, 'Halt the men, Sergeant-Major. Send them back.'

It was Norton. The soldiers had him over a barrel and he knew it. Stifling his anger, he offered them the top rate and, to show there were no hard feelings, threw in an extra 1s 9d (9p) ration money for that day's food.

Hill 60

As the new tunnelling units were hurried across the Channel in late February, the army was already preparing a nasty surprise for them. Their first target had been chosen, the sinister Hill 60. On 8 March work began on three tunnels: M1, M2 and M3. Garfield Morgan was put to work on M3, with a starting point just behind British lines and only 150 feet (45 m) from the German trenches. The first day wasn't good. As Garfield and his

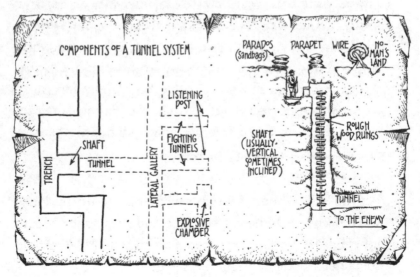

Plan of a tunnel

mate Albert Rees started work on the shaft, they uncovered the rotting body of a French soldier. In the next two hours they exposed three more corpses and, trying desperately not to be sick, tipped them into body bags. After dark they dragged them back for burial in a grave lined with **quicklime**.

Working round the clock in eight-hour shifts, the miners drove the tunnels forward 10 feet (3 m) a day. The thick Flanders clay was perfect for 'clay-kicking', but if the digging was trouble-free, other perils lay in wait. Although the tunnels were lined with stout timber boards, liquid mud burst through the joints in powerful jets. Worse, ventilation rapidly became a problem. When the air turned fetid, the only air pumps available were left over from the Crimean War – 60 years earlier! These noisy antiques were almost useless and had to be replaced with a hastily rigged system. Large bellows, like those in a blacksmith's shop, were used to blow fresh air down a hosepipe to the men hacking at the clay.

But the flow was never enough. Candles would grow dim and splutter out, while matches glowed a strange cherry red without bursting into flame. Lack of oxygen gave the miners blinding headaches and their chests heaved and wheezed in an eerie roaring noise. Many were dragged to the surface blue and gasping for breath long before their shifts had finished. In M3 Garfield sustained lasting damage to his eyes.

All the work had to be done in near silence to avoid

discovery. The miners talked in whispers, while tools were used gently and iron parts muffled in cloth. Even so, the Germans suspected something was up. Listening posts tried to detect the noise of the British excavations, while enemy engineers set off explosives to shake the tunnels down. Every day the miners faced the risk of being killed by concussion or by being buried alive in a tomb of their own making.

In early April Garfield and Albert were working at the face of M3a (a branch of M3) when Albert felt his shovel break through into ... nothing. With his spade waggling in thin air, he called Garfield over to look at the ragged black hole on the left-hand side of the tunnel. Turning quickly, he snuffed out the candle just in time to hear footsteps splash by on the other side of the cavity. It was a German tunnel! Shocked, they scrambled back to find an officer.

An hour later they were back with Second Lieutenant Thomas Black. In pitch darkness the three men slowly edged along the tunnel until they came to the hole. No sooner had Thomas switched on his electric torch, than ... CRACK ... a bullet ripped through the sleeve of his uniform. This sent them clawing their way back along M3 to the safety of the shaft entrance, their ears ringing from the boom of the gun firing in such a cramped space. When the miners plucked up courage to return a second time they found a canister of German explosives wired to fire. They cut the leads and replaced the enemy

German miners

device with their own huge charges of **guncotton**. But what would happen next? With M3 and M3a discovered, the success of the attack rested on the two other tunnels.

Boom Time

By Saturday 10 April the digging at Hill 60 was almost finished. M1 and M2 extended 300 feet (90 m) beneath no man's land, before splaying out into four smaller branches under enemy lines. Now the last and most dangerous job lay ahead: bringing up the explosives. Major David Griffiths, the officer in charge of the operation, calculated he needed 4 tons of gunpowder to blow up Hill 60. That meant over 90 bags of powder, each weighing 100 lb (45 kg) to be carried from the rear trenches by hand.

The miners worked in teams of three to lug their deadly loads – two men to lift a bag on to the shoulders of the third, with a stop every 300 feet to change over. Night after night they risked the terrifying journey, slipping and sliding on muddy duckboards. Only black humour relieved the screaming ache of their muscles – just how many pieces would they be blown into if a stray shell landed nearby?

At last the gunpowder was winched down the shafts and hauled to the end of the tunnels. Behind the charges sandbag walls were built 10 feet (3 m) thick to make sure the blast went upwards towards the enemy. In case of problems, two fuses were laid to waterproof the ignition charges in each tunnel – simple burning fuses and high-tech electrical wires running back to plungers. By 15 April everything was ready for zero hour.

The last 48 hours were a nightmare of waiting. Every inch of fuse was checked every two hours in case of breaks, the miners crawling in the dark with their flashlights. Alarmingly, German digging could be heard above M1 and M2. It was clear the enemy now had their own tunnels and a race was on. Were they almost ready to blow their mines too? No one could be sure.

After a long winter, 17 April was a fine spring day. There was sunshine and a warm breeze. As evening drew on, the shelling subsided, as if both sides were settling down for a pleasant rest. In the unusual quiet, the British mines were detonated at 19:05.

The explosion lasted for 10 long seconds. Hill 60 burst open like a volcano, and debris was flung 300 feet into the air. Mud, sandbags and bodies rained down. The shockwaves left the German survivors dazed and helpless. A British artillery bombardment began at once and the infantry went over the top. In less than 15 minutes the battered remains of Hill 60 were in British hands.

FIGHTING FACTS

Holding On

The course of war is rarely clear and the British soon discovered that taking Hill 60 was the easy part. Keeping it became a nightmare. The hill and the shattered ground around it were a tiny wedge – only 750 feet (230 m) long and 600 feet (180 m) wide – poking into German lines. It was exposed to enemy fire from two sides and by 20:00 that same evening accurate German gunners were already pounding the site. During that first night there were four ferocious counter-attacks – and the enemy kept coming. Over the next three days four Victoria Crosses (medals) were won by courageous soldiers as the British clung on desperately to a killing field. After the war one historian called Hill 60 'a rubbish heap in which it is impossible to dig without disturbing a body'.

Gas

The first British infantry on Hill 60 sent back a series of alarming reports. Some men had collapsed, gasping for breath, convinced they had been gassed. And they were right – they had been gassed by accident! The Germans had been planning an attack with this frightening new weapon and were positioning cylinders of chlorine when the British fired their mines. Some of the cylinders had cracked and the gas leaked slowly out. Unfortunately, in the heat of battle, the reports were ignored. It seemed more likely to the authorities that the men had been affected by fumes from bursting shells or from the gunpowder in the mines. A vital warning had been missed.

On 22 April 1915 the Germans launched the first gas attack on the Western Front, against French troops holding the line north of Ypres. Newly arrived Algerians were the first to breathe the deadly fumes and fell back in panic, choking and vomiting.

At 08:45 on 4 May the exhausted defenders on Hill

60 spotted a dense bluish cloud drifting towards them. With only cotton pads to press to their faces, there was little they could do. Shortly after the gas swirled into the British trenches a fierce German assault retook the broken hill. One victim was Garfield Morgan, who staggered back towards Ypres, clutching his throat and throwing up bright green vomit. It took him 11 weeks in hospital to recover.

Messines Ridge

In June 1917 the British began the third Battle of Ypres – one more attempt to break through the German lines in Belgium. What made this attack unique was the use of mines of unimaginable power. Nineteen tunnels were dug altogether, a total length of $4^1/2$ miles (7 km), and charged with 500 tons of explosive.

The tunnelling had started 18 months earlier and was finished a year before the assault. The work was carried out in the strictest secrecy and silence. Lieutenant Bryan Frayling of 171 Tunnelling Company remembered: 'We wore felt slippers, used rubber-wheeled trolleys on wooden rails and spoke in whispers.'

Even so, the enemy was active, listening for the British and digging their own counter-tunnels. Sometimes, when German workings were detected, a small mine would be fired to destroy them – hopefully without damaging the British tunnels too much. And of course the Germans were trying to do exactly the same. It was a tense battle of wits and timing, with the miners never knowing if they were about to be buried alive. And sometimes, if a tunnel was vital, the British weren't allowed to hit first. Lieutenant Frayling commented:

> The Germans were down below and every now and again gave us trouble. When the Germans 'blew' us we never answered back, we suffered casualties and did nothing, tried not to give away where we were. We listened for them with very delicate instruments, like the geophone. One of our officers was once so near to a German shaft that he wrote down and translated a series of yarns that the German NCO told his shift.

Finally, at 03:10 on 7 June, the mines were fired – 17 detonating simultaneously. The noise, a drawn-out roar, was heard hundreds of miles away. A captain in the Royal Engineers wrote:

> It seemed as if the Messines Ridge got up and shook itself. All along its flank belched rows of mushroom-shaped masses of debris, flung high in the air. Gradually the masses commenced to disintegrate, as the released gases forced their way through the centres in pillars of flames. Then along the enemy line rolled dense columns of smoke, tumbling into weird formations as they mounted into the sky.

More horribly, Lieutenant Frayling noted:

The flames went up higher than St Paul's. I estimated about 800 feet. It was a white incandescent light, we knew that the temperature was about 3,000 degrees centigrade. The Germans there went up as gas. The biggest bit of a German I found afterwards was one foot in a boot.

German resistance on the ridge collapsed and by 05:00 it was in British hands. Over 7,000 prisoners were taken, together with 48 guns and 218 machine guns. The assault was a rare success. Unfortunately, the main attack went ahead three weeks later and became bogged down in

The ruins of Ypres, 22 November 1916. This battered city came to symbolize the plight of the Belgian people

frightful weather around the village of Passchendaele – the name by which the battle became better known. More than 300,000 British and Empire troops were killed or injured.

Missing Mine

Only 17 mines were detonated on 7 June 1917? Yes, you're right – two were missing! One was discovered in 1955 and blown up. The other is still down there . . . deadly and undiscovered.

Hanging on the Old Barbed Wire

If you want to find the old battalion,
I know where they are, I know where they are,
I know where they are.
If you want to find the old battalion,
I know where they are.
They're hanging on the old barbed wire.
I've seen 'em, I've seen 'em,
Hanging on the old barbed wire.
I've seen 'em, I've seen 'em,
Hanging on the old barbed wire.

Trench song

GALLIPOLI – A SIDE SHOW

BATTLE BRIEFING

The Lure of Constantinople

By 1915 it was clear that victory on the Western Front would be hard won. There had already been nearly a million Allied casualties. Horrified by the killing match in France, powerful voices in the British government began to look round for easier options. 'Why,' they argued, 'hammer at the front door of the enemy if we can sneak up from behind?'

Winston Churchill, the First Lord of the Admiralty, had his own pet scheme: to pick off one of Germany's newest allies, Turkey. And he believed he was in charge of just the service to do this quickly and cheaply: the Royal Navy. Churchill proposed that a fleet of battleships should smash through Turkish defences on the straits of the Dardanelles and threaten Constantinople (today known as Istanbul). This, he argued, would bring a host of advantages to the Allies.

Turkey and Gallipoli peninsula, 1915

War-winning Advantage 1

The Turkish government, which supported Germany, would be thrown out and replaced by Turks who would back the Allies.

War-winning Advantage 2

Other countries in the area, such as Greece and Bulgaria, would look to the Allies for leadership and threaten Austria-Hungary, Germany's partner.

War-winning Advantage 3

Hard-pressed Russia would be able to export grain through

the Black Sea and earn money to pay for her armies on the Eastern Front.

You can see the geographical importance of Turkey from the map on page 49. No wonder breaching the Dardanelles seemed like a magical solution to the war!

A Gamble on the Fleet

And it almost came off. By February 1915 the strongest fleet ever seen in the Mediterranean was stationed off the straits. A British officer wrote: 'It looked as if no human power could withstand such an array of might.' In softening-up operations, Turkish forts were shelled and anti-ship mines cleared until the British admiral, de Roebuck, judged the time was right to attack.

On 18 March, a hot spring morning, a combined force of 18 British and French battleships, guarded by an armada of cruisers and destroyers, began to fight their way through. Several ships were hit, but they suffered little damage and by 14:00 the Allies were almost 10 miles (16 km) into enemy waters and going well. The bombardment had shaken the Turks and their official version of the action states:

> All telephone wires were cut, all communications with
> the forts were interrupted, some guns had been
> knocked out and others half buried, others again were
> out of action with the breech mechanism jammed.

Then abruptly the tide of battle turned. The French

battleship Bouvet *hit a mine and vanished in less than a minute, with the loss of almost 600 men. By 18:00 two more battleships had been sunk by mines and three seriously damaged. Shaken by losing a third of his force, de Roebuck pulled out. In the coming days he glumly decided that the Dardanelles could not be cracked open by ships alone. Troops had to land on the Gallipoli peninsula and knock out the enemy guns. Little did he know that by nightfall on 18 March, the Turks were almost out of ammunition. One more push would have seen his fleet within firing range of Constantinople.*

The Army Steps In

The very idea that troops might be needed to support the navy caused weeks of fierce argument in the British government. It wasn't until mid-March that Field Marshal Kitchener, the Secretary of State for War, agreed. After that everything happened in a messy rush. Sir Ian Hamilton was given command of the Mediterranean Expeditionary Force (MEF) to Gallipoli, but left England with almost no idea of what he faced. He had no detailed maps, no information about the enemy and no battle plan.

Sir Ian took his first look at the Gallipoli peninsula from the deck of the battleship Queen Elizabeth *– and he was daunted. The terrain was bleak, a gnarled finger of hilly land 50 miles (80 km) long, riven by steep ravines. He reported to Kitchener, 'It looks a much tougher nut to crack than it did over the map in your office.'*

This was the understatement of the year! From the start, Gallipoli was a ramshackle campaign and this woeful situation was to cost thousands of lives ...

V BEACH

Making Do

To crack open Gallipoli, Sir Ian was given a force of 75,000 troops, largely the British 29th Division and the Anzacs (the Australian and New Zealand Army Corps). The troops trained briefly in Egypt before moving to the Greek island of Lemnos for the final attack. Sir Ian made his plans at breakneck speed but surprise was the last thing he could hope for. Every move the MEF made was watched by Turkish spies and reported to Constantinople.

Sir Ian was well aware that his men faced the toughest of jobs – landing from the sea against an enemy dug in and waiting – and yet they had arrived without the most basic supplies. His list of urgent worries ran like this:

- My men don't have enough ammunition.
- They have no grenades.
- They only have a handful of mortars.
- Worst of all, there are no landing craft to get them ashore!

*

To Sir Ian's fury, the landing craft were ready and waiting, but in England. There was a small fleet of armoured barges, built for an **amphibious attack** in the Baltic – an attack that never happened. However, when he asked for them he was curtly refused. Instead, MEF officers had to scour Egypt to buy every spare tug and small boat for the landings, every donkey for transport, and every skin, and every oil drum and kerosene tin to hold water.

Sir Ian threw his efforts into the landing plans. How and where, he pondered, would he get enough men ashore to set up a **bridgehead**? And how would he trick the Turks so they didn't wipe out his men on the beaches? By mid-April the details were ready.

The British Plan

The main assault force, the 29th Division, would punch inland from three tiny beaches at the tip of Cape Hellas. They were codenamed X, W and V. The landing commander was to be General Hunter-Watson.

To divide and confuse the Turks, 2,000 men would hit Y beach further north (see map on page 54), while the Anzacs would storm ashore at Gaba Tepe, Z beach.

Sir Ian was convinced that once the British were on land the enemy would crumble. And his men agreed. An Australian private summed up the cocky mood of the army when he wrote home: 'Who could stop us? Not the bloody Turks!'

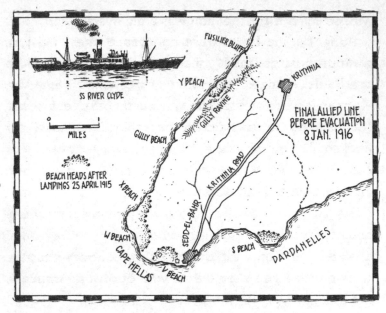

British landings at V beach

The final date set for the landings was 25 April, only a few weeks since Sir Ian had been given the job. Amazingly fast. But not fast enough.

Tough Turkey

Like a team briefing before a football match, the British had studied the form of the Turks – and didn't rate them. They would soon crumble, like the native armies thrashed in dozens of wars across the Empire. And a close look at a Turkish unit would have done nothing to change this opinion. Many soldiers wore tattered uniforms, with shoes made from rags and tied together with string. But this opinion was a big mistake.

As far as the Turks were concerned, they had just given the greatest navy in the world a bloody nose. And they were ready to hand out more punishment. The German general Otto Liman von Sanders was given command of the defences on the Gallipoli peninsula and worked his own miracle.

The Turkish Defence

Troops scattered thinly round the entire coastline were pulled back to form mobile reserves.

At the same time the defences around every possible landing site were strengthened with new, deep trenches and barbed wire.

Liman von Sanders gleefully wrote: 'The British allowed us four weeks of respite for all this good work before their great disembarkation [landing] . . . this was just enough.'

With every day that passed the Gallipoli nut got tougher.

Robert Unwin's Brainwave

The British knew that the success of the operation depended on landing plenty of men fast and swamping the Turks. But without landing craft what could be done? The navy came up with a plan. Warships would transport the troops to within a mile of the beaches and then ferry them ashore in strings of small boats called 'tows'.

Each tow would be hauled by a powered tug. It was risky but there was no alternative.

Thinking the problem through, Commander Robert Unwin had a brainwave. He reckoned he could go one better than the tows and use a merchant ship to land extra men in the first wave of the attack. They would go in on the key landing zone: V beach.

Robert was a seasoned Royal Navy officer and commanded the destroyer *Hussar*. Given the go-ahead, he created a secret weapon that was soon compared to the ancient Greek trick, the Trojan Horse. An innocent-looking collier (coal carrier), the *River Clyde*, was converted into an armoured landing craft. Carrying 2,000 men in her hold, she would be rammed into V beach. The troops would pour out from four large holes – or **sally ports** – cut through her steel plates and dash down gangways supported by ropes. The gangways led to a bridge made from barges lashed to the shoreline. These barges were to be towed alongside the *River Clyde* and manoeuvred into place as soon as the collier ran aground.

V Beach

The task force, over 200 ships, had gathered at Lemnos and began to move off on 23 April. By midnight on the 24th most warships, with the assault troops aboard, had reached their battle stations. Still out of sight of land, they came to a stop, and a meal of hot coffee and rolls was given to the soldiers. For many it was a last taste of luxury.

At first light, around 05:00, the assault troops got their first glimpse of V beach. It wasn't inviting. The landing zone was shaped like the sides of a bowl, with a small gravelly beach around 1,000 feet (300 m) long and 100 feet (30 m) wide. Behind this the ground rose steeply, with low cliffs on the left and a ruined fort above the village of Sedd-el-Bahr on the right. Tiers of trenches and thick rows of barbed wire ringed the beach. Unseen, but deadly, the Turks had four machine guns and two 37-mm pom-pom guns set to give a murderous crossfire.

The assault began when the battleship *Albion* opened fire to soften up the defences. For 30 minutes V beach was pounded. A little after 06:00 the *River Clyde* began her run-in, packed with 2,000 men from the Munster Fusiliers, the Dublin Fusiliers and the Hampshire Regiment. Alongside ran a tow of around 20 small boats carrying over 700 Dublins. Each man carried an 80-lb (40-kg) pack and there was little room to move. When the naval fire subsided an eerie quiet fell over the tiny bay. Surely the Turks were either dead or their morale broken? Perhaps they had taken to their heels? A staff officer on board the *River Clyde* jotted in his notebook, '6.22 a.m. Ran smoothly ashore without a tremor. No opposition. We shall land unopposed.'

But the Turks had not run away. The bombardment had barely touched their trenches or barbed-wire entanglements. They watched, waited and held their fire until the British grounded. The Dublins, in their fragile open boats, took the first deadly fusillade. Only around 300 survived the deadly machine guns to make it to the beach and many of them were wounded. Desperately, they hid behind a sand bank about 30 feet (10 m) in, helplessly pinned down. Major David French wrote:

> *One of the men close to me fell dead – shot. I realized that having practically wiped out those in the three boats ahead they were now concentrating their fire on us. I jumped at once into the sea (up to my chest) yelling at the men to make a rush for it and follow me. But the poor devils – packed like sardines in a tin – could scarcely clamber over the sides and only two reached the shore un-hit. The water seemed to be alive – the bullets striking the sea all around us.*

To those watching from the comparative safety of the *River Clyde* it seemed as if the Dublins were 'slaughtered like rats in a trap'. Meanwhile, the attack from the collier had its own problems.

Leaving the Clyde

When the *River Clyde* hit V beach Captain Guy Geddes, commanding a company of Munsters, noted, 'None of us felt it, there was no jar.' But there was no way off either. The steam-powered barge that was supposed to make the bridge between the ship and the shore veered to port (the left) and ran aground in the wrong place. Robert Unwin grimly realized that it was up to him to save the landing.

Shells bursting near SS *River Clyde*, V beach, Gallipoli, 1915

Since the *River Clyde* was his idea, Robert was acting as captain on the old collier that day. He left the bridge at once and dived into the sea with a rope, followed by Able Seaman William Williams. Together they lashed a couple of lighters (flat-bottomed boats for unloading ships) into position to make a causeway. But there was nothing to fasten the boats to and so no way to stop the swift current running along the coast from whipping them away. With every second vital, Robert and William decided that they would have to become living anchors to keep the boats in place.

Braced in the sea, while machine-gun bullets thrashed the water around him, Robert tied the boats to himself. A little behind, William added his weight to the line. Once secure, they yelled for the soldiers to start the landing. Gamely the men poured out of the sally ports and down the gangways – straight into the enemy guns. The massacre of the Dublins had finished minutes before and now the Turks concentrated their fire on the *River Clyde*. Soon the gangways and the causeway were choked with the dead and dying. The sea turned red with the blood of the wounded who fell overboard and drowned under the weight of their packs. Those who reached the shore dodged and slithered their way to the flimsy protection of the sandbank.

The sailors held the boats as long as they could, but soon William was hit. To stop him from drowning, Robert let go of the rope and the lighters began to move.

British troops storm ashore under heavy Turkish machine-gun fire

At just this moment Guy Geddes led his men out:

We got it like anything, man after man behind me shot down, but they never wavered. Lieutenant Watts, who was wounded in five places and lying on the gangway, cheered the men on with cries of 'Follow the Captain'. Captain French of the Dublins told me afterwards that he counted the first 48 men to follow me and they all fell ... I stepped on to the second lighter and looked around to find myself alone. I jumped into the sea and had to swim a dozen strokes to get ashore.

By this time 51-year-old Robert was exhausted and collapsed. He was taken back aboard the *Clyde* to recover and his place was taken by three other brave sailors. After less than an hour's rest he was back in the water, holding the causeway in place again. Robert Unwin and William Williams were awarded the Victoria Cross for their actions. Amazingly, Robert survived the day, but William died of his wounds shortly after he was hit.

By 09:30 over 1,000 men had charged out of the *River Clyde*, yet more than half were killed or injured before they reached the beach. Finally, the officers called off the assault, now gloomily sure that nothing more could be done until nightfall. Those left on board settled to wait as best they could in the baking heat of the hull. They had one comforting thought as they sweated out the rest of the day: at least for now the steel plates of the ship sheltered them from the enemy guns.

With good reason the Turkish commander, Colonel Mahmut, was elated. He had held the bay with only a few dozen men and proudly reported:

> The shore became full of enemy corpses, like a shoal of fish. The enemy troops were so frightened that they refused to disembark from the large transport (the River Clyde). Their officers had drawn swords and were sending men down the ladders but they were observed and could not escape our Turkish bullets.

The Second Wave

General Hunter-Watson was stationed on board the Cruiser *Euryalis*, five minutes' sailing time from V beach. But, far from knowing that the attack had collapsed, he believed all was well. At 07:50 the general was told that British troops were already in Sedd-el-Behr and moving forward. Buoyed up by this good news, he ordered the second wave, led by Brigadier General Napier, to go in at 08:30.

Impatiently Napier walked the deck of the troop transport, which in kinder days had been a cross-Channel ferry. 'Where are those damn boats? They should have returned by now,' he muttered. Then the tow came into view. Only half a dozen boats had living crews and most were packed with dead or wounded soldiers. The weary sailors said nothing. It was not their job to decide if the landing was hopeless. And Napier didn't ask their opinion.

Hastily the boats were cleared, but there were too few to carry more than the brigadier general, his staff and a few men. Nevertheless, the general was determined to get ashore and sat down carefully on the slippery, blood-soaked seats. As the tow returned to the beach at around 09:30 an astonished officer on the *River Clyde* couldn't believe his eyes. He grabbed a megaphone and called to Napier to come alongside. 'You can't possibly land,' a chorus of voices warned. But the brigadier general was made of sterner stuff. From his place in the lead boat he could see the causeway from the *River Clyde* to the shore full of men, pinned down by Turkish fire. What they needed was an example – firm leadership.

'I'll have a damned good try,' he yelled back, and sprang on board the lighters with his staff. Only then did he realize the soldiers were all dead. Seconds later, the machine guns chattered again. Napier and those with him were cut down before they could reach the beach.

FIGHTING FACTS

Bridgehead
No more men landed on V beach during daylight on 25 April but as dusk fell the remaining soldiers aboard the *River Clyde* came ashore in small parties. Second Lieutenant Gillet described the horror that met them:

A panoramic shot of the Gallipoli beachhead packed with supplies

The barges, now linked together and more or less reaching the shore, were piled high with mutilated bodies – and between the last barge and the shore was a pier formed by piles of dead men. It was impossible to reach the shore without treading on the dead, and the sea round the cove was red with blood.

Although there had been chaos at V beach, the other landings fared better and a fragile bridgehead was set up. On 26 April Turkish troops pulled back to new defences across the peninsula in front of Krithnia and the scene was set for a brutal slogging match that lasted for months. Sir Ian was relieved of command on 15 October and the new commander, General Monro, recommended

evacuation. By 9 January 1916 the British and their allies had pulled out of Gallipoli.

Fortunes of War

War is often about missed opportunities. In February 1915 the battleship *Vengeance* pounded the ancient fort at Sedd-el-Bahr and the Turkish guns were wrecked or abandoned by their crews. A party of Royal Marines and sailors landed without any trouble. They strolled up the beach to the fort and blew up undamaged guns and smashed searchlights. Satisfied with their work they left – with no sign of the Turks. As you have just read, when the British came back two months later the scene was tragically different.

Statistics from Gallipoli

Nationality	Casualties	Killed
Australian	26,094	7,594
New Zealand	7,594	2,431
British Empire (other than Australia and New Zealand)	171,335	119,335
French	47,000	27,000
Turkish	251,309	86,000

A Dirty War

In the eight months of fierce fighting that followed the Gallipoli landings, living conditions for the British troops at Gallipoli were dirty and squalid. More men fell sick than were killed or injured in battle. Read on and shudder!

Dirty Heat

Cool weather lasted throughout May and wild flowers bloomed everywhere, even between the front lines. But by July the temperature had soared to 84 degrees Fahrenheit (29°C) in the shade – for the fortunate few who could find any shade in the arid landscape. It was so hot that the fat melted in tins of bully beef and metal plates were too hot to touch.

Dirty Water

Except for a couple of springs and some wells dug by

engineers, there was no drinking water in the Cape Hellas bridgehead. Most had to be brought in from Egypt, 700 miles (1,100 km) away, and rations were often down to 3 pints (1.8 litres) a day each for drinking and washing. Lieutenant-Colonel Burge wrote:

> The only thing there is to drink is water that comes from a well, which tastes as if it had a dead mule in it (it probably has). However, we are given purifying tablets, which are very good and make the water taste as if it had two dead mules in it.

Dirty Food

Gallipoli rations: bully beef, army biscuits, apricot or plum jam and tea without milk.

Occasional treats: rum, bread, condensed milk.

Fresh food: throw a hand grenade into the sea and collect the stunned and dead fish.

A Gallipoli Recipe:

Take two or three hard biscuits
   (supplied by Huntley and Palmers)
Bash with entrenching tool (small shovel) till pulverized
Mix with water to make flour
Roll into ball in khaki handkerchief (preferably unused)
Boil in water in mess tin

It was horrible but at least it was different!

Dirty Lice

Most soldiers fought three wars in Gallipoli: one against the Turks, the second against blood-sucking lice and the third against fleas. The lice infested their clothes, and drove men wild with itching and scratching. Here's a list of the troops' main ways of dealing with these tiny foes:

1. Nip 'em and squeeze 'em.
2. Burn 'em out of the seams of your clothes with candles or hot embers of the fire (try not to scorch the cloth).
3. Keatings flea powder. Problem: they seem to like it.
4. Army-issue camphor balls. Problem: they make nests in them.
5. Most ingenious weapon (promote this man to sergeant): Lay clothes over an ant's nest (there are a lot in Gallipoli) for the ants to feed on the lice. It works! But be sure to shake all the ants out, their bite is far worse than a louse's.

Dirty Flies

Think about this – but not for too long. Thousands of dead bodies, sometimes in bits, and tens of thousands of men using open ditches as toilets! Then add a plague of flies – not just a couple buzzing against the window on a hot summer's day but billions of them. The flies arrived in June and fed on the corpses, the latrines, the rubbish and the food. Ivone Kirkpatrick remembered:

*I used to cover the top of a box with sugar and kill flies
en masse with a sort of home-made ping-pong racquet,
but although I often went on killing till I was tired, it
never seemed to make much difference.*

Dirty Diseases

With the flies came dysentery. Imagine having violent
and crippling diarrhoea – and no proper toilets, toilet
paper or any way to keep yourself clean. By July 1915
over 1,000 men a week were so ill that they had to be
evacuated to hospitals.

Other diseases prevalent at Gallipoli were jaundice,
malaria and typhoid.

Last Man Down

The last Gallipoli veteran died in May 2002, aged 103.
Australian Alec Campbell lied about his age and joined
up when he was 16. He was one of 50,000 Anzacs
among the British-led Allied army. Alec braved heavy fire
to carry water and ammunition to the front line. He
remembered: 'It was dangerous work. Every day at least
one carrier got hit. Once we were there we didn't
expect to survive.'

The memory of the Gallipoli campaign is so important
to Australians that Prime Minister John Howard cut
short a trip to China to attend Alec's funeral service in
Tasmania. The whole country came to a halt to observe
a minute's silence at 11:00.

I Want to Go Home

I want to go home, I want to go home.
I don't want to go in the trenches no more,
Where whizzbangs and shrapnel they whistle and roar.
Take me over the sea, where the **Alleyman** can't get at
    me.
Oh my, I don't want to die, I want to go home.

I want to go home, I want to go home.
I don't want to visit la Belle France no more,
For Oh the **Jack Johnsons** they make such a roar.
Take me over the sea, where the snipers they can't get
    at me.
Oh my, I don't want to die, I want to go home.

Trench song

GUESTS OF THE KAISER

BATTLE BRIEFING

Prisoners of War

*While there are many stories of Allied prisoners in World War II, the **POWs** of World War I have been largely forgotten. Yet the total number of prisoners taken was huge, about 6.6 million. On the Western Front the Germans captured some 170,000 British soldiers and 500,000 French. On the Eastern Front many more Russians became reluctant guests of the Kaiser, including 92,000 in one week during the Battle of Tannenburg in August 1914.*

The belligerents promised to follow the rules of war agreed to at the conventions of Geneva (1907) and The Hague (1908) and take reasonable care of captured enemy soldiers. In reality the long and bitter struggle often led to the mistreatment or neglect of prisoners. Life in the camps was dreary and hard, with poor food and contagious diseases, such as typhus, rife. Inmates were expected to work – to cover some of the costs of their detention – in mines, farming, factories or public services. One British prisoner at a camp in Tournai listed the many jobs he was given: 'making railways, emptying coal barges, cleaning streets, removing shells from trucks, carrying German wounded from the trains to hospital.'

Soldiers never expected to be taken prisoner and the moment of capture always came as a shock. In April 1915 Canadian Baron Richardson Racey could never have guessed that his days of freedom were almost over ... or that his diary would tell one of the great escape stories of the war. The words in italics are his.

ESCAPE RECIPE

January 1916: Vehnemoor Prison Camp

It was a hard march to the new prison camp, 10 miles (16 km) from the station through the freezing January weather. That night Baron scribbled a quick entry in his diary: *Finally arrived more dead than alive, ate a basin of fish soup and crawled to bed on the hard boards.*

Baron kept his diary well hidden from the guards. It was his lifeline. When fits of the 'blues' left him cursing his bad luck and wondering if the war would ever end, the diary was an escape route in his head. But even

Baron had to admit that some days it made dismal reading. That night, as the cold bit through his thin blankets, those last days of freedom seemed so long ago. So full of 'if onlys' ...

April 1915: Ypres

Baron was among the first contingent of Canadians to arrive in Belgium, a private in the Royal Montreal Regiment. Looking back, the night No. 3 Company moved up to the front at Ypres seemed like an omen. It was mid-April 1915, pitch black and pouring with rain. They stumbled forwards along a long a road that was nothing but shell holes, swearing in whispers as one man after another tumbled into the muddy craters.

When they finally reached their position – the reserve trenches – life didn't improve. The dugouts were so small and cramped that the first man through the low door jammed tight, trapped by his own bulky kit. The whole company was held up while he was dragged clear by his pals, half smothered. It would have seemed funny if the odd shell hadn't been zipping overhead.

The Canadians soon learned that trench life was **nocturnal**. All the next day they were under strict orders to keep their heads down. So far German gunners hadn't located the reserve lines, and to keep it like that, if they moved they crawled. As soon as darkness fell Baron and the others set to work on new dugouts. But it was a grim experience.

The ground was like a huge graveyard and we were continually unearthing dead Germans. One chap dug up a bugler and somebody got the bugle as a souvenir and very quickly buried the **squarehead** *again, I can assure you.*

Digging was thirsty work, but water from nearby streams was undrinkable. Bottles had to be carried from the battalion water cart at St Julien, about a mile away. No fires were allowed so there was no *beloved tea* or hot food. Stew was brought up from the cook wagon, *but by the time it arrived it was stone cold with about an inch of grease on top.*

Gas Attack

A few days later the Montreals were relieved and Baron enjoyed a break in Ypres, marvelling at the battered remains of the Cloth Hall and enjoying the company of a pretty Belgian girl. But the fun didn't last long. A Jack Johnson exploded nearby and she dived into a cellar for cover. The romance over, Baron hurried back to his unit.

There was chaos everywhere. Batteries of horse-drawn artillery galloped past, hysterical civilians ran around in panic and, most ominous of all, he saw dozens of French soldiers stumbling along, gasping for breath. This was 22 April and Baron was in the middle of the first big German gas attack on the Western Front (see pages 42–3). The Algerians holding the line had broken, leaving a gap 4 miles (6 km) long. As the Germans poured through, the Canadians moved up to plug the breach.

It took hard-nosed courage to advance through the fleeing French. Like their allies, the Montreals had no protection against this new weapon. Baron wrote:

All we could get out of them was 'les Allemands vient avec le gaz asphixiant' [the Germans are coming with poisonous gas] and then they would burst into a fit of the most awful choking and stagger on a few more yards.

Around St Julien the Canadians dug in like the *busiest little moles.* Baron had just finished his foxhole when he was ordered forward with two others to locate the enemy position. Inching ahead for 600 feet (180 m) they lay in a ditch and listened carefully. German voices? Yes!

Job done, the trio started back, one at a time. Baron was last, around 120 feet (37 m) behind the others, when a stern French voice demanded to know who he was.

Now, hindsight is a wonderful thing! And the if onlys ran through his thoughts for months afterwards.

If only I'd kept quiet.

If only I'd run.

If only I'd opened fire.

Like a damned fool, thinking they were a stray party of French, I told them in broken English and French who I was, but got the shock of my young life when about a dozen spiked helmets jumped up at me. One grabbed my rifle and another my bayonet . . .

In less than the time it takes to tell, he was a prisoner.

Captivity

Baron's first night in German hands was spent locked in a barn with two dying Algerians. They had been badly gassed, and groaned, choked and coughed their lives slowly away. To add to their hellish rattle, two **batteries** of German guns moved in behind the farm buildings and opened fire. By dawn he was nearly deaf from the roar.

Next morning Baron and about a dozen others were marched back through the captured French lines. The memory burned vividly:

A lovely spring morning and then you stumble across a mangled heap of human beings, or at least all that remained of them, some perhaps showing no wounds at all, as if they were asleep; others hunched up into all kinds of strange shapes.

And soon he got his first taste of enemy hospitality – *a damned rough time.* Some German soldiers dashed out of their billets to look at the 'Englanders', jeering and yelling insults; others thought the chance too good to miss, spitting on and kicking the prisoners as they passed. In the coming months the treatment didn't get any better.

Newly captured British POWs held in a field

The next night was spent locked in the church in the village of Staden. Officers came and went, taking photographs and asking questions, but at least they didn't hand out beatings. One old general strolled across to Baron and asked him for his Royal Montreal badges for souvenirs. Feeling it would be ill-mannered to refuse, he handed them over. By now desperate for sleep, he crawled into a confession box and got his head down.

The following day the humiliation continued. The prisoners were lined up in a column of fours to march to the station, but no sooner had they left the church than waiting German troops closed in, baying like a pack of dogs. Marching on the outside of the row, Baron was kicked black and blue. But worse was to come. At the station, the men were packed tight into cattle cars for transportation to prison camp – 60 to a car. There was no room to sit or lie down and among them were more gassed and seriously ill Algerians – many vomiting or suffering from diarrhoea. The journey took two days, and the train stopped only once for a 10-minute toilet break.

A line of British POWs being sent to prison camp in cattle trucks

Camp Memories

Following his capture, Baron was locked up in four camps, each leaving sharp memories.

Camp 1

Meschede in Westphalia, Prussia, where the 'Englanders'

78

were given all the worst jobs, like cleaning the drains and emptying the camp rubbish. Lunch was always soup – black bean and potato soup, dried fish and potato soup or sauerkraut and potato soup, Supper was a German delicacy – salt herring, absolutely raw. Baron noted ruefully:

> Men who had money were able to buy sausage,
> margarine and honey at the canteen. I sold everything
> I had and was dressed in rags. A tunic would fetch
> anything from five to ten marks and boots up to 20.
> I sold my hat, tunic, watch, but hung on to my boots.

Parcels sent from home or by the Red Cross were essential for extra food, luxuries and new clothes (see page 96).

Feeding prisoners. The man on the right of the large pan is using his helmet as a bowl

Camp 2

In July 1915 Baron was moved to Giessen, near Frankfurt, and with great regret staged a mini-rebellion. He was among a party of prisoners sent to live on a farm and help with the work. The farmer was kind, the food good and it was great to be away from the camp.

So why spoil it?

Baron's reasoning went like this:

> *We had a great discussion as to whether it was right for us to work for the Germans ... helping them with their food supply. Half a dozen of us talked it over and decided to strike.*

The Germans were furious. The prisoners were denounced as *'nichts arbeiters'* – 'won't works' – and sent straight back to camp to the punishment barracks. This meant eight hours a day standing to attention or sitting still on a stool: no cigarettes, food parcels or books – and no talking. If anyone nodded off, the guard would gleefully pour a jug of cold water down his neck.

Camp 3

Just after New Year 1916 came Cellelager in Hanover. The food was better ... well, at least the soup seemed thicker. But the camp, built on flat and swampy ground, was dismal beyond description. Baron was there only a week ... yet soon he wished it had been longer.

Camp 4

Then Vehnemoor, near Oldenburg. It made him shudder at first sight. The place was ankle deep in mud and the barracks were filthy. Three hundred prisoners were crammed in each block, sleeping in bunks three tiers high. Through the wire fence, there was nothing to see but miles and miles of bleak, waterlogged moor. For the first time Baron began to think seriously of escape.

Escape or Die

Getting out of the camps seemed the easy part. Baron had witnessed quite a few breaks for freedom, some by fellow Canadians. Yet most escapees were soon recaptured and brought back to kick their heels in the punishment cells. Why did so many attempts go wrong? For the rest of that miserable winter he made it his business to find out.

Scouring the camp, Baron chatted to every prisoner who had gone over the wire and learned important lessons from each adventure:

- If you break out in a big group split up quickly. Pairs are best.
- Stay hidden during the day.
- Take your time at the frontier. Don't get too impatient. Choose the right spot and wait.

Armed with these golden rules, Baron prepared to head for the nearest border, neutral Holland. But how was he to find the way? Little by little, he begged, borrowed and stole a bespoke escape kit:

- Compass: the essential item! Bought from a Russian for 15 marks and several shirts and sets of underwear.
- File: stolen from a workshop.
- Railway timetable with small map of Germany: generously given by another prisoner.
- Oilskin and water-wings: sent from home in a parcel. Amazingly, the Germans didn't confiscate the water-wings or even ask how much swimming practice he expected in a prison camp!
- Food: saved from Red Cross parcels.

By the spring Baron was all set, when prison life took another sudden dive. That Easter, he was sent with around 50 others to Schwansburg Bei Friesoythe to work on a huge potato farm. OK, it was 20 miles (32 km) away – 20 miles nearer the Dutch border. But that was the end of the good news.

The prisoners were met with a shocking sight when they marched into the old factory that was to be their new barracks. Baron wrote:

The building was occupied by about 50 Russians who were the most pitiable objects, their clothes in rags, no boots, just wooden sabots with no socks and straw stuck in them. Pale, lifeless-looking specimens, just existing from day to day. They had been in this camp two years, living

on a starvation diet and working like slaves all day. They
even had to put grass in their soup to thicken it and
dozens of them had died the previous summer.

The condition of the Russians was a warning; this camp was to be the most brutal yet.

The guards woke the prisoners at 06:00 with cries of '*Raus, raus, austand*', lashing out with sticks or rifle butts. Anyone sick was beaten out of bed and dragged along. The work was back-breaking: planting or carrying sacks of potatoes until it was hard to stand upright. No food parcels reached them for a month and the meals were dire. To survive, Baron was forced to eat his precious escape stocks. But one memory burned most of all:

Our work was superintended by a German civvy who
was strongly inoculated [sic] with hate of all Englanders
... he used to bring out his wife at lunch time to see
'the swine eat', as we heard him telling her. I only hope
it is my good fortune to get him alone in the
backwoods ...

Breakout

By mid-July Baron had squirrelled away new escape rations and found three willing partners: Harry Ramsay, Adzich (a **Montenegrin**) and Lovell. They planned to make a break together and then split up into pairs at the River Ems, before trying for the frontier. Every night for a week they slept with their clothes on, ready to run. Finally the night of 13 July was perfect – heavy rain and pitch black. Baron had been watching the guards on patrol for weeks and knew they had a 'gateway' between rounds.

When everyone was asleep, the budding **Houdinis** crept to the back of the barracks, through a chorus of snores and grunts. To keep the noise down each man wore three pairs of heavy socks over his boots. Kneeling

Baron Richardson Racey (second left) in the oilskin coat he was wearing when he escaped

by the back wall, they squeezed though a hole – made earlier by loosening two boards – into an adjoining outhouse. Scanning again for the guard, they edged through the door and took it in turns to climb on to the roof of the outhouse. This gave them the height they needed to jump over the perimeter wire.

Adzich went first, making such a racket that the others thought the game was up. But their luck held. He cleared the wire and dashed to the rendezvous point, a nearby shepherd's hut. Baron jumped third, leaping clear of the roof, but catching the seat of his trousers on the wire. Like a manic acrobat he dangled, wriggling furiously until his trousers tore loose. Even the loud RRRRRIP of

Escaping over the fence

cloth and TWANGGGG of wire failed to bring the guards running.

Escape Highlights
Once clear of the camp it was time to move fast, travelling at night and hiding by day. When the novelty of being free wore off, the journey became a test of endurance and nerves.

Night 1
Cloaked by lowering clouds and filthy weather, Baron and his mates headed towards a small hill, seen in the distance from the camp. At about 04:00 they took cover in a hayfield. Breakfast was a feast: bully beef and biscuits.

Scariest time: Germans working in the fields around them, so close they dare not sit up.

Night 2
As dark fell, they pushed on hard across open moors. The waterlogged ground was an obstacle course of ditches and streams. At daybreak they hid in thick woodland near a village. Baron had good cause to write about this day, as it was his birthday: *We sat down to the strangest party I shall ever experience. Instead of cake we ate some fudge sent me from a friend in Toronto.*

Scariest time: The woods were next to a main road. They could hear Germans talking as they rode past in carts.

Night 3

Shortly after the village settled down for the night the escapees crept through, armed with thick clubs made out of branches. Stopping at intervals to check the compass, they travelled on to the edge of a small town. Skirting this through fields, they crossed a main road that showed on their tiny map. Perfect! Only a few miles from the River Ems and bang on target for Holland. Relieved, they took refuge in a field of wheat for the day.

Scariest time: Being spooked by horses or cows during their night march. Baron noted: *Your heart would be in your mouth until you realized what it was, and the relief would be intense.*

Night 4

The prisoners reached the River Ems but decided to rest up before trying to cross. They slept in a wood again and, since supplies were almost gone, their meal was half an Oxo cube each and a few mouldy crumbs.

Scariest time: Two hunters out shooting rabbits almost stumbled into their hiding place.

Night 5

This was an action-packed night that quickly became a comedy of errors. Adzich, faced with crossing the Ems, admitted he couldn't swim a stroke, while Lovell complained he would get 'cramps' if he tried to swim without the help of the water-wings. There was an anxious pause for planning.

Then Harry came up with a bright idea: they could build a raft! He and Lovell tore down two field gates and cut fencing wire to bind them together. Instant raft. And Baron, being the lightest of the four, had the 'fun' of taking her for a maiden voyage. It was short and wet. The raft worked, sort of – it would carry one person if they didn't mind being partly submerged. Troubles over? No, they were just beginning ... Now this bit is complicated, so read carefully.

Blunder 1
Baron and Harry stripped and swam across the Ems, using the raft to keep their clothes dry. Except the clothes fell off and got soaked anyway.

Blunder 2
Lovell swam across using the water-wings, picked up the raft and went back for Adzich. Except he lost the raft halfway back and began to panic.

Blunder 3
Baron and Harry saw a man running along their side of the bank, flapping his arms and yelling. It was Lovell – making enough noise to attract every German patrol for miles. They calmed him down, ready to go back again for Adzich. Except the water-wings burst – and Adzich was stuck!

Blazing Row

At this point, all their anger and frustration erupted and the three men had a blazing row.

Lovell's argument: We can't desert Adzich. We must stick together, find a bridge and go and get him.

Baron's argument: All the bridges will be guarded. We might as well surrender as try to cross one. You lost the raft. Adzich is your problem.

As Baron drily wrote, *after mutual compliments had passed between us, Lovell started along the bank.* It was time to split up.

That day Baron and Harry hid in a swamp near the river ... in sopping-wet clothes ... in the pouring rain ... with no food ... and with very large slugs that crawled all over them.

Night 6

The intrepid pair travelled due west, using the stars as a guide. The border was achingly close now and sentries frequent.

Scariest moment: Caught in the open by a patrol, Baron and Harry hugged the ground, taking an hour to wriggle slowly past. Then the moon came out and the 'patrol' turned into *blocks of peat piled up about the height of a man.* Oops!

The next day dawned hot and dry. They camped in a field of rye and seized the chance to take their sodden clothes off and dry them. Their bellies rumbled but they fought off the hunger pangs by smoking the day away.

Night 7

Time for the final push to Holland – on a brilliant moonlit night.

Good point: They could see clearly.

Bad point: So could any Germans.

Checking the compass, they headed due west, across a small canal and a main road, crawling or sticking tightly to the shadows cast by tall hedges. Coming to a crossroad, Baron and Harry could hear yells and see lights flashing. With seconds to spare, they flung themselves into a ditch and lay still as a patrol marched past, rifles slung.

After a brief wait they crawled into a field and over some low mounds. Harry stopped and gave Baron a kick. The mounds were freshly dug graves! As if to prove the point, shots rang out in the dark and someone gave a bloodcurdling yell. Sentries dashed to and fro. Was it some other poor devil heading for the border? Taking a chance, they sprinted for cover in the garden of a nearby house. Problems enough, you'd think, but then Harry whispered, 'For God's sake, look over the hedge.' Glinting in the moonlight were two anchored airships. They had blundered into a makeshift German aerodrome.

Baron and Harry spent the rest of the night huddled in a shrubbery until dawn, when another shock awaited them. The house had been converted into the airfield HQ. All the glass in the upper windows had been taken out and a wooden platform had been built on the roof. This had a gun mounted on it. If they were caught now they were likely to be shot as spies, never mind rearrested as escapees.

In a desperate situation they fell back on the boldest of plans. Waiting till local workers were on the move, they stood up and walked out of the garden. Trying to look part of the scenery, the pals coolly lit cigarettes and strolled behind two men carrying dinner pails. Incredibly it worked. They were given a few suspicious glances but no one stopped them. Some friendly civilians even grunted 'Good morning' and seemed content with the '*Ja, ja*' Baron growled in return.

The rest of the day was spent heading west, always looking for quiet lanes. At a railway crossing a soldier walking the tracks stared at them, but let them go unchallenged. Why, Baron couldn't guess. Even to his eyes they seemed shady: *Two awful-looking scarecrows – nine days' beard, not washed, sleeping anywhere in mud, clothes torn by barbed wire.*

At last they sat down by a wood and Baron picked up a scrap of newspaper – the language was Dutch. They looked in astonishment. Had they crossed the border without even realizing, or had the paper blown some distance? There was only one way to check. When an old farmer ambled past with a few cows, they stepped out and asked in German which country they were in, Germany or Holland. '*Nederland*,' came the reply.

The farmer watched in amazement as the two scarecrows danced in the road. They'd made it!

FIGHTING FACTS

What Happened to Baron?

Baron survived the war fit and well. It was Canadian army policy not to send prisoners back to the front, so he returned to civilian life as a bank clerk. With the war still raging, he was eager to join up again and made repeated applications to the new Naval Air Arm. By the time he had been taken on for pilot training, however, the fighting in Europe was over.

In World War II Baron was back in uniform, as a major in the Veterans Guard of Canada, and in a way fate turned full circle. He found himself the commanding officer of an internment camp for Austrian Jews, refugees held in camps in case they were enemy agents. Needless to say, his own experiences gave him plenty of sympathy with their plight.

What Happened to Lovell and Adzich?

Did you think that Baron was a bit hard on Lovell and Adzich when they split up? Well, you can stop worrying.

Baron Richardson Racey, c 1942

By a stroke of luck, Lovell found a boat about a quarter of a mile away and got Adzich across the river. They made it to Holland too.

Young Lions

When Britain went to war in 1914 the peoples of the Dominions, Canada, Australia, New Zealand and India, joined the struggle. The Canadian record was remarkable. From a population of only 8 million, 619,636 men and women joined up. Of these 66,655 were killed, while another 172,950 became casualties.

The fighting spirit of Canadian troops was second to none. During the deadly German breakthrough on 22 April at Ypres, they counter-attacked and held the crumbling line until reinforcements arrived. Two days later the Germans struck again and this time their target was the Canadians. As the gas cloud billowed over, the defenders were left gasping for air through mud-soaked handkerchiefs, but they were not driven back. The cost, however, was high: 6,035 Canadian men died – one in three of those in the battle.

Red Cross Aid

The International Committee of the Red Cross (ICRC), based in neutral Switzerland, tried to make sure warring nations followed the rules of the Geneva Convention. Red Cross officials visited hundreds of POW camps and checked the standards of food,

A recruiting poster appealing for help from the Empire

hygiene and prisoners' quarters. The ICRC had no powers to force countries to improve conditions, but it could try to embarrass them into better treatment by making its reports public.

From the prisoners' point of view the Red Cross organized one marvellous service – parcels of food, clothing and other luxuries – and they'd sent out almost 2 million by the end of the war. A food parcel was designed to weigh 13 lb (6 kg) and soldiers could expect to be sent two every fortnight. Each one was like a mini Christmas present and included cocoa, tea, cigarettes, biscuits, cheese and tinned milk.

For many prison inmates, including Baron, they made the difference between health and malnutrition. Baron recalled his many hunger pangs:

The first card I sent home simply said, 'I am a prisoner' and, well, the second one was filled up with request for grub. You could bet your boots if you saw a party of Englishmen talking together the subject was GRUB with a capital G, either describing with full details the last large juicy steak they had, or the last Christmas dinner . . . I used to dream of maple sugar and buckwheat pancakes.

Parcel Problems

Parcels were often searched, because early in the war there had been cases of families and friends hiding escape kits: files or saws in packets of sugar or compasses in tins of cigarettes. This had made camp commandants uneasy, especially if they were close to the Dutch border. Later, it was common for guards to steal parcels. By 1918 there were severe shortages in Germany and many civilians were close to starvation. Women and children were even seen begging through the barbed wire for food from prisoners. Parcels were also used to punish prisoners: bad behaviour, no parcels.

Did the Germans Really Hate British Prisoners?

Baron complains bitterly of German harshness towards British prisoners, but was their treatment really worse than average? He may have a point! Early in the war German troops disliked the British because they were professional soldiers or – even worse – volunteers, not conscripts like themselves. In the eyes of some, this made them little better than mercenaries (hired killers). Later in the war, when the Royal Navy blockade led to widespread food shortages in Germany, British soldiers were blamed. One wounded prisoner remembered that, as he lay on the operating table, he was asked what kind of soldier he was. When he replied that he was a regular, the surgeon said, 'Good. If you had been a volunteer I would not have operated on you.' So you can well imagine what the Germans thought of Canadian volunteers who had sailed 3,000 miles to get into a European war!

However, if the Germans disliked the British it was the Russians they really detested. So many Russian prisoners fell into German hands that they couldn't cope and tens of thousands died of malnutrition or from diseases such as dysentery. The condition of the Russians seen by Baron was all too typical.

Bombed Last Night

Bombed last night, and bombed the night before.
Going to get bombed tonight if we never get bombed
　any more.
When we're bombed, we're scared as can be.
Can't stop the bombing from old Higher Germany.

They're warning us, they're warning us.
One shell hole for just the four of us.
Thank your lucky stars there are no more of us.
So one of us can fill it alone.

Gassed last night, and gassed the night before.
Going to get gassed tonight if we never get gassed any
　more.
When we're gassed we're sick as can be.
For phosgene and mustard gas is too much for me.

They're killing us, they're killing us.
One respirator between the four of us.
Thank your lucky stars that we can all run fast.
So one of us can take it all alone.

Trench song

THE PRISONERS' MARTYR – EDITH CAVELL

BATTLE BRIEFING

A Women's War

World War I transformed the role of women in Britain. Although they were not called up and did not fight, they did play a vital support role in the war effort. About 1.5 million women went into industry to replace the men who had joined up and to supply the vast range of equipment the armed services needed, everything from uniforms and rifles to artillery and ammunition. They took on a host of jobs – as engineers, carpenters, plumbers, crane drivers, munitions workers and bus or tram conductors – often tackling skilled work done only by men before.

Other women, however, wanted to get closer to the action and help the men who were suffering. Between 1914 and 1918 around 23,000 served as nurses and 15,000 as orderlies of the Voluntary Aid Detachment. Most worked in military hospitals in England but several thousand served in field hospitals close to the front lines and saw the full cost of the war. They dealt with men whose limbs had been shattered by shellfire or whose lungs had been seared by poisonous gas.

Not surprisingly, some nurses broke down under the stress of the horrors they witnessed and were forced to leave. But most found a way to cope and stayed, buoyed up by a sense of duty. In 1915 one story became an inspiration for a whole generation of young women.

EDITH CAVELL

A Sense of Duty

In early August 1914 Edith Cavell was in Norwich on a short holiday from her nurses' training college in Belgium. She had come to visit her elderly mother and was enjoying the warm summer weather. Edith was in the garden, digging weeds, when she heard the news that excited all Europe: war had been declared and German troops were massed on the Belgian border. Her response was instant: 'At a time like this I am needed more than ever.' Protests from friends and family fell on deaf ears.

Edith Cavell in uniform

Edith knew where her duty lay. She must return to
Brussels as soon as possible ... whatever the risks.

Duty was the thread that ran through the life of Edith
Louisa Cavell. Born in 1865, she was the daughter of the
vicar of Swardeston, a small village in Norfolk. Although
the Cavells lived in an imposing vicarage, keeping up

appearances was not easy and money was always short. One disgruntled maid scribbled on an attic bedroom wall: 'The pay is small, the food is bad, I wonder why I don't go mad.' Even so, the family shared what they had. When Sunday lunch was served a portion of the joint was always sent to poor and hungry villagers.

The situation of the Cavell family meant that Edith had to earn her own living. At 16 she began training as a pupil teacher and showed a gift for French. Three years later she became a governess – a respectable job for a middle-class girl. After working with English families for a few years, Edith's sense of adventure led her abroad. In 1890 she took a job with the François family in Brussels and enjoyed life in Belgium. In 1895, however, her father became seriously ill and she returned home to nurse him – sowing the seed for the next change in her life.

A Caring Career
Edith had been looking for a greater challenge, a career that would allow her to help more people, and at the age of 30 she decided to go into nursing. It was not an easy choice. In 1896 she began training at the London Hospital under the stern eye of Eva Lückes. Hours were long, 07:00 to 21:00, with only half an hour for lunch. And Edith did not impress her tutor. Miss Lückes observed witheringly: 'Edith Louisa Cavell had plenty of capacity for her work, when she chose to exert herself . . . she was not at all punctual.'

The following year, however, Edith redeemed herself. She was part of an emergency team of six nurses sent to help with an outbreak of typhoid fever at Maidstone. Thanks to their care, out of 1,700 patients who caught the disease, only 132 died.

In 1907 Edith's Belgian connections led to an offer she couldn't refuse. Dr Antoine Lepage was trying to set up a new school to train nurses at the Berkendael Institute near Brussels and he needed an able matron who could speak French. Edith was recommended to him by one of the François children, now grown up and married, and he eagerly interviewed her. An English nurse who could bring the ideas of Florence Nightingale to Belgium would be perfect.

The job was a challenge. As in England a generation before, Belgian mothers from 'good families' were horrified at the idea of their daughters becoming nurses. It took time, hard work and patience to break through this snobbery. One reason for Edith's success was her dedication to her work. Students remembered her as a brisk and businesslike woman in her forties, with high expectations. She kept a watch on the table in front of her at breakfast, and any girl more than two minutes late would be ordered to work an extra two hours. By 1912 the Berkendael Institute had become a modern teaching hospital, providing nurses for three other hospitals, 24 schools and 13 kindergartens.

War Zone

That fateful August in 1914 Edith quickly returned to Brussels and shared the nightmare that hit the Belgian people over the next few weeks. The German army invaded on 4 August; by the 16th the mighty Liège forts had been stormed; Brussels was captured on the 20th; and the British army sent reeling back from Mons on the 23rd. One bewildered German soldier wrote:

> *When one sees the wasting, burning villages and towns, plundered cellars and attics, dead or half-starved animals, cattle bellowing in the sugar beet fields and then corpses, corpses, corpses ... then everything becomes a lunacy.*

With heavy fighting nearby, the institute became a Red Cross hospital, meaning that wounded from both sides could be treated without the staff facing repercussions.

Soon after Brussels fell, the Germans ordered 60 British nurses to return home, but Edith and one English assistant, Sister White, were allowed to stay behind and continue their work with their Belgian staff. The German authorities believed that since Edith was working under the banner of the Red Cross, she would remain strictly **neutral**. But within weeks she was forced to choose between her conscience and her neutrality. During September a young Belgian engineer called Herman Capiau visited Edith. He told her a harrowing tale: dozens of British soldiers trapped behind enemy lines had been sheltered by Belgian civilians, but at great risk. The Germans, determined to cow the Belgians into submission, were hunting down these stragglers and sometimes shooting them, together with any civilian who had dared to hide them. Warily, Edith agreed to help liberate these soldiers.

A piecemeal **resistance movement** soon sprang up to fight back against this harsh rule. The Prince and Princess de Croy, together with a trusted group of brave Belgians, built an escape network to help British soldiers get across the border to Holland. Since the only hope of liberating Belgium lay in an Allied victory, the more men they sent back to the war the better. But, just as importantly, they assisted many Belgian and French men of fighting age to flee the German-occupied zones and join up. The network password was Yorc – Croy backwards.

Going Underground

On 1 November Herman Capiau put Edith's offer to the test. Now a key worker in the de Croy organization, he urgently needed a bolt hole for two British soldiers. Like many others, Lieutenant-Colonel Dudley Bolger and Company Sergeant-Major Frank Meachin, both from the Cheshire Regiment, had been cut off as the British army retreated from Mons. They had been lucky enough to be taken in by an elderly woman, Mrs Libiez, who hid them in an outbuilding in her garden for several weeks – until an informer tipped off the Germans. Dudley and Frank escaped just in time. They managed to slip out of the back door and mingle with crowds of local civilians just as a company of **Landsturm** cycle troops swooped on their hideout.

A desperate game of hide-and-seek began as the network passed the soldiers from **safe house** to safe house. And into the hands of Herman Capiau. On a grey and dismal autumn night, Herman led them through the streets of Brussels to the Berkendael Institute. German patrols seemed to be everywhere, but their disguises worked. Dudley wore the black hat and floppy tie of an ordinary Belgian factory worker, while Frank flamboyantly squashed rolls of cloth between his shoulders blades, so he looked like a hunchback. This way, if anyone asked why a tall, well-built man was not in the army he had a ready excuse.

It was a little before 20:00 when the three arrived on Edith's doorstep, but it never crossed her mind to turn them away.

'These men are fugitive soldiers,' she told Sister White. 'Give them beds in the empty surgical house.'

Exhausted and dirty, but highly relieved, Dudley and Frank were soon sound asleep in crisp white sheets.

Edith hid the escapees for two weeks – until she had warning that the Germans were going to search the institute. Sister White took them to an empty house on the nearby Avenue Louise, where they stayed before being moved on. Finally, a guide escorted them out of the city, to the canal path leading to Ghent. Frank was lucky. He made friends with a Belgian who smuggled newspapers across the border from Holland. With the smuggler's help, he reached the frontier and dashed to safety. Dudley was caught when a German patrol searched a café where he had stopped to have a drink. He was sent to a prisoner of war camp at Ruhleben, Germany, and spent the rest of the war behind barbed wire.

Belgium, Holland, France and Germany

For Edith this deadly adventure was just the beginning. Frank and Dudley were the first of more than 200 fugitives she sheltered at the institute in the coming months.

Arrest

In May 1915 Edith received heartbreaking news. The liner *Lusitania* had been sunk by a German submarine and her friend Madame Lepage had drowned. She was the wife of the doctor who founded the institute and was returning from a fund-raising mission to the USA. This toughened Edith's resolve to fight on, but already the network was starting to unravel. The Germans were suspicious and the evidence was mounting.

In an act of incredible stupidity, a group of British soldiers sheltering at the institute had sneaked out to a nearby café and got drunk. Everyone in the neighbourhood now knew what was going on and some tongues wagged. Compounding this, one soldier who made it back to England sent Edith a postcard ... with his thanks!

Worst of all, one escapee helped by the network turned out to be a **collaborator** and the institute was searched several times. Coolly, Edith had sewn up her diary in a cushion to avoid detection.

On 31 July 1915 the end came suddenly. The house of Philippe Baucq, a key figure in the network, was raided. Philippe was detained and incriminating letters, with

Edith's name in them, were seized before he could destroy them. Shortly afterwards, Prince de Croy visited Edith with alarming news: he was going into hiding, before fleeing to Holland, and she should do the same. Her reply was forthright: 'I expect to be arrested. Escape for me is futile and unthinkable.' Perhaps it was stubbornness, perhaps her sense of duty, perhaps a dogged urge to defy the Germans, but Edith did not run.

On 5 August the Germans came for her, led by Otto Mayer of the secret police. After three days of intense questioning, the German interrogators tried a new approach. 'We know everything,' they told her. 'Thirty-five members of the network have been arrested and they have confessed. We will go easy with them if you cooperate.'

Naively, Edith believed what she was told and made a full confession, pouring out names, dates and places. Later she wrote in a letter: 'Had I not helped they would have been shot.'

Edith was locked up in the prison of St Giles until her trial before a German military court in October. The United States Ambassador in Belgium, Brand Whitlock, scornfully described what such trials were like:

The secret police would bring before the bench of German officers all the evidence as they called it ... The court would admit hearsay, presumptions, inferences and innuendoes so long as they were on the part of the prosecution. The accused was sometimes allowed to present a defence but it was only such as he might contrive in sparring with the judges.

Edith came to trial on Thursday 7 October, alongside the others who had been rounded up. The court sat for just 48 hours but the judges were impressed by Edith's forthright honesty. When asked if she had helped 20 soldiers to escape she replied, 'Yes. More than 20, 200.'

'English?'

'No, not all English. French and Belgians too.'

But her courage was not the issue. In the eyes of the army judges Edith had committed treason. On Monday 11 October they pronounced her sentence: death by firing squad, to be carried out the next day at the Tir Nationale, the National Rifle Range. But she was not to die alone. Philippe Baucq would be shot alongside her. That night she told Stirling Gahn, the English priest allowed to visit her, 'I know that patriotism is not enough. I must have no hatred and no bitterness towards anyone.'

Edith and Philippe were woken at dawn and driven to the execution ground in an army motor car. Edith was wearing her white nursing uniform. The firing squads presented arms and the sentence was read out in German and French. Philippe yelled in a clear voice, 'Comrades, in the presence of death we are all comrades.' He was not allowed to say any more. A

German chaplain, Pasteur Le Seur, comforted Edith. He recalled:

> I took Miss Cavell's hand and said in English, 'The Grace of our Lord Jesus Christ and the love of God and the Communion of the Holy Spirit be with you for ever. Amen.' She pressed my hand in return and answered, 'Ask Mr Gahn to tell my loved ones that my soul, as I believe, is safe, and that I am glad to die for my country.' Then I led her a few steps to a pole, to which she was loosely bound. A bandage was put over her eyes which, as the soldier who put it on told me, were full of tears.

Seconds later the shots rang out and Edith's body slumped forward. One bullet had gone through her forehead. Death was quick.

FIGHTING FACTS

Outrage

Although the German execution of Edith Cavell was justified according to the rules of war, it was a costly mistake. Both the American and Spanish ambassadors had pleaded for her life, stressing the way she had helped the wounded of both sides, but they were ignored. When the news of Edith's execution broke,

MURDERED

OCTOBER 12TH, 1915

By THE Huns

MISS EDITH CAVELL

ENLIST IN THE 99th

AND HELP STOP SUCH ATROCITIES

PUBLISHED BY THE ESSEX COUNTY RECRUITING COMMITTEE

The execcution of Edith outraged Britain and led to angry posters like this

public opinion across the world was outraged. The USA became more sympathetic to the Allied cause, while in Britain recruitment doubled for eight weeks after her death was announced.

Today the memory of Edith Cavell is still honoured. In 1919 her body was brought home and buried in Norwich Cathedral. Each year a memorial service is held to recall her bravery and sacrifice. In Canada Mount Edith Cavell, a mountain in the Jasper National Park, Alberta, was named in tribute to her.

Gallant Little Belgium

On 2 August 1914 Germany demanded the right to march a huge army through Belgian territory to deliver a knockout blow against France. When this was refused the Germans invaded anyway, on the night of 3–4 August. It was this attack on a small, neutral country that brought Britain into the war. Lord Baden-Powell, the founder of the Scout movement, summed up the public mood when he compared Belgium to a plucky little tailor set upon by 'a big beery loafer'.

During the war Belgium suffered terribly. The German attack was fast and brutal. The ancient university library at Louvain went up in flames, while 600 civilians were shot at Dinant after snipers fired on passing German troops. When the capital, Brussels, fell on 20 August the government moved to Antwerp and finally to Le Havre in France. Before the end of October 1914, most of the

Recruiting poster

country was occupied and a million civilians became refugees, with over 100,000 fleeing to Britain. By 1917 many of those who had stayed behind were desperate. In Brussels alone, one third of the 750,000 people living in the city were penniless and kept alive only by soup kitchens.

Eyewitness: A Nurse's View

Edith was not alone during the dreadful weeks of 1914 when most of Belgium was conquered. Dozens of British nurses were close to the fighting. One published her diary anonymously in 1918, with the title *Sketches from a Belgian Field Hospital*. She served through the siege of Antwerp and left this moving description of evacuating wounded from the shattered city in a London bus commandeered by the army:

> *Have you ever ridden in a London motor bus? If not, I can give you little idea what our poor wounded suffered. To begin with, even traversing the smooth London streets these vehicles jolt you to bits, whilst the smell of burnt gasoline is stifling, so just imagine these unwieldy things bumping along over cobblestones and loose sandy ruts of rough tracks among the sand-dunes. When you have the picture before you just think of the passengers – not healthy people on a penny bus ride, but wounded soldiers and sailors. Upon the brow of many, death had set his seal. All those inside*

passengers were either wounded in the abdomen, shot through the lungs or pierced through the skull, often with their brains running out through the wound, whilst we had more than one case of men with broken backs. Many of these we had just operated upon.

My Boy Jack

'Have you news of my boy Jack?'
Not this tide.
'When do you think he'll come back?'
Not with this wind blowing and this tide.

'Had anyone else had word of him?'
Not this tide
For what is sunk will hardly swim,
Not with this wind blowing, and this tide.

'Oh, dear, what comfort can I find?'
None this tide,
Nor any tide,
Except he did not shame his kind –
Not even with that wind blowing, and that tide.

Then hold up your head up all the more,
This tide,
And every tide;
Because he was the son you bore,
And gave to that wind blowing and that tide!

Rudyard Kipling

AFTERMATH

The Unknown Warrior

When World War I came to an end, Britain was a nation in mourning. With 743,00 dead and over 1,500,000 injured, almost every family had suffered terribly. Yet some faced an extra agony – the relatives and friends of men who simply vanished. Every battle left thousands of bodies so badly disfigured they couldn't be identified, while other soldiers were simply blown apart by artillery fire. One famous father who never recovered from the loss of his only son, 'My Boy Jack', was the author Rudyard Kipling. Jack's body was never found and Rudyard spent years interviewing survivors to try and trace him.

In 1919 the suggestion was made to bring home the body of an unidentified soldier for reburial in Britain. This would become a national memorial and a symbol for all the others who had no grave. The original idea came from the vicar of Margate, the Reverend David Railton, a former army chaplain who had served in France. Years later he recalled the poignant moment in 1916 that inspired him:

I went to a billet in front of Erkingham, near Armentières. At the back was a small garden and in the garden, only six paces from the house, there was a grave. At the head of the grave there stood a rough cross of white wood. On the cross was written in deep black-pencilled letters, 'An Unknown Soldier' and in brackets beneath 'of the Black Watch'. It was dusk and no one was near, except some officers in the billet playing cards. I remember how still it was. Even the guns seemed to be resting. How that grave made me think . . .

It took a year for the War Office to agree but in 1920 the plan went ahead. Brigadier General Wyatt, the officer who had commanded British troops in France and Flanders, chose the body. Four unidentified corpses were dug up and brought to the chapel at his HQ at St Pol. They came from four battle areas – the Aisne, the Somme, Arras and Ypres. Each body was draped in a Union Jack and laid on a stretcher. Wyatt pointed at one and helped to lift it into a plain, inner coffin. The other three were reburied in a nearby military cemetery.

The next day, 9 November, the Unknown Warrior began his journey home. The simple coffin was placed in a magnificent oak sarcophagus, cut from a tree in the grounds of Hampton Court Palace. On top was fixed a crusader-style sword presented by King George V.

In memory of their joint losses, a guard of French cavalry escorted the Unknown Warrior to Boulogne. There he was placed on a British destroyer, the *Verdun*, for the journey across the Channel. The warship had been named in tribute to the hard-fought battle that cost the lives of 160,000 Frenchmen.

As the *Verdun* arrived in Dover, a nineteen-gun salute rang out. Crowds gathered at every station on the line to London to watch the train carrying the body steam past. The *Daily Mail* reported, 'The train thundered

Bringing the Unknown Warrior to England from Boulogne, 11 November 1920

The King placing a wreath on the coffin of the Unknown Warrior at the Cenotaph

through a dark, wet, moonless night. At the platforms by which it rushed could be seen groups of women watching and silent, many dressed in deep mourning.'

On the morning of 11 November 1920 the coffin was placed on a gun carriage and drawn by six black horses to Whitehall. There, on the last stroke of 11:00 the King unveiled the new **Cenotaph,** designed by the architect Edward Lutyens. As the chimes died away the crowds fell silent for two minutes and the last post sounded.

The war correspondent Philip Gibbs captured the mood of many ex-soldiers when he wrote:

It did not seem an unknown warrior whose body came down Whitehall. He was known to us all. It was one of 'our boys' – not warriors – as we called them. To some women weeping a little in the crowd after an all-night vigil, he was their own boy who went missing and was never found till now. To many men wearing ribbons and badges in civilian clothes he was one of their comrades.

The solemn procession continued to Westminster Abbey, where the nave was lined with the greatest guard of honour ever seen in Britain – 100 holders of the Victoria Cross. In contrast to this military splendour, the congregation was mainly widows and

The ceremony to seal the grave of the Unknown Warrior in Westminster Abbey

Veterans at the Cenotaph today

grieving mothers. As the coffin was placed in the grave the King scattered it with soil from the battlefields of France. By the time the grave was finally closed, on 18 November, over 1 million people had visited the abbey to pay their last respects.

The Casualties

Countries	Total Mobilized	Dead	Wounded	Prisoners & Missing	Total Casualties	Casualties % of Mobilized
Allied Powers						
Russia	12,000,000	1,700,000	4,950,000	2,500,000	9,150,000	76.3
France	8,410,000	1,357,800	4,266,000	537,000	6,160,800	73.6
British Empire	8,904,467	908,371	2,090,212	191,652	3,190,235	35.8
Italy	5,615,000	650,000	947,000	600,000	2,197,000	39.1
United States	4,355,000	126,000	234,300	4,500	364,800	8.4
Romania	750,000	335,706	120,000	80,000	535,706	71.4
Serbia	707,343	45,000	133,148	152,958	331,106	46.8
Belgium	267,000	13,716	44,686	34,659	93,061	34.9
Central Powers						
Germany	11,000,000	1,773,700	4,216,058	1,152,800	7,142,558	64.9
Austria-Hungary	7,800,000	1,200,000	3,620,000	2,200,000	7,020,000	90.0
Turkey	2,850,000	325,000	400,000	250,000	975,000	34.2
Bulgaria	1,200,000	87,500	152,390	27,029	266,919	22.2

FIGHTING FACTS

War Poets

Between the chapters there is a trench song or a poem
– a tiny sample of the thousands written during and
after the war. With millions of men and women in

combat, there was a stunning outburst of creativity as people struggled to make sense of their experiences. If you want to find out more, search for 'Trench Songs' or 'War Poets' on the Internet. Look out for authors such as Siegfried Sassoon, who won the Military Cross and suffered from shell shock; Wilfred Owen, who was killed on 4 November 1918, just one week before the war ended; or Robert Graves, who also wrote one of the best wartime biographies, *Goodbye to All That*. Most of the soldiers' songs are anonymous, but you'll notice how funny, ironic and often very rude they are. They reflect the bravery and steadfastness of the armed forces of the British Empire throughout the four years of bitter fighting.

All Over Again

Twenty-one years after World War I ended, World War II broke out between Britain and Hitler's Germany. Old soldiers joked that the bell had sounded for round two. This time the fighting spread over many countries in Europe, Africa and the Far East. It took six long years before peace came again.

Commemoration on the Web

Do you have a relative who died in World War I? You can keep alive their memory by looking them up on the *Debt of Honour Register* compiled by the Commonwealth War Graves Commission at www.cwgc.org/.

TRENCH TALK

barrage artillery bombardment.

Blighty army slang for Britain. A 'blighty one' was a wound bad enough to get a soldier sent home.

Boche rude nickname for the Germans, picked up from French soldiers

bully beef tinned corned beef, the main source of protein in a soldier's rations.

Fritz British nickname for the Germans.

exaspirator nickname for a gas mask.

Hun unsavoury nickname for a German, after the barbaric Huns of history.

Jack Johnson nickname for the fearsome German 150-mm heavy howitzer shells, infamous for their noise and black smoke. Johnson was the first black American heavyweight boxing champion, from 1909 to 1915.

Maconochie tinned meat and vegetable stew, named after the packing company. A top medal for bravery was the Military Medal or MM. Troops joked this was the Maconochie Medal, a reward for eating the stew.

mess tin a metal dish that was used as a plate, cup and cooking pan.

Montenegrin a person who lives in Montenegro, a small country in the Balkans that fought on the Allied side.

morning hate (or evening hate): an exchange of artillery fire by both sides, often at dawn or dusk.

no man's land neutral ground between the two front lines.

potato masher a German stick grenade.

puttee a cloth strip wound round the leg from ankle to

knee as a legging.

squarehead Canadian nickname for German soldiers.

star shell a shell that explodes high in the air, lighting up the landscape at night to detect sneak attacks.

Tommy German nickname for a British soldier.

whizzbang a light shell, it went whizz ... and then bang.

GLOSSARY

Alleyman a German. Taken from the French for Germany, *Allemagne*.

amphibious attack an assault from the sea.

batteries fortified emplacements for heavy artillery.

belligerents countries at war.

billets somewhere to rest, perhaps with a Belgian family or at least a dry tent.

bridgehead ground captured from the enemy after an attack from the sea.

cenotaph war memorial or memorial to someone buried elsewhere. Cenotaph is Greek for 'empty tomb'.

collaborator native of an occupied country, such as Belgium or France, working for the Germans.

commandeered seized by the army. The owners were paid compensation.

'Deutschland, Deutschland über

Alles' the German national anthem.

Dominions self-governing colonies of the British Empire.

dugout a rough shelter, often dug into the side of a trench. Sometimes referred to as a funkhole.

fire steps the ledges cut for soldiers to stand on and fire at the enemy.

guncotton nitrocellulose, an explosive.

Houdinis Harry Houdini was a magician who specialized in great escapes.

Kaiser German emperor and war leader.

Landsturm part-time German reserve soldiers, a bit like the Home Guard in World War II.

Mills bomb grenade.

mobilize to gather an army together.

neutral to not take sides in the war.

NCO non-commissioned officer. A soldier from the ranks, appointed to lead others – like a corporal or sergeant.

nocturnal active at night.

oilskin waterproof coat.

orderlies attendants in military hospitals, cleaning and doing basic nursing work.

outflank get behind and cut off part of the enemy army.

parapets bank or wall to protect soldiers from enemy fire.

phosgene poisonous gas used by both sides. It had a nasty delayed action, causing sudden death as long as two days after exposure. It was common for a victim not to realize he had been gassed.

POWs prisoners of war.

quicklime caustic calcium oxide powder, used as a disinfectant.

resistance movement civilians organizing opposition to the conquering power.

safe house property that was safe from the enemy where fugitives could be hidden.

salient the front line sticking out into enemy territory.

sally ports holes cut in the sides of ships to let the troops out.

sapper a private in the Royal Engineers.

skirmish small battle.

U-boat German submarine. Taken from *Unterseeboot*, which means 'under-seaboat' in German.

ACKNOWLEDGEMENTS

Many thanks to Richard Racey for permission to retell his father's amazing escape story and for his kindness in checking the manuscript.

Picture Credits

IWM: p.11 Q2314 p.21 Q70165 p.31 Q44172 p.45 Q6209 p.59 Q61088 p.64–65 25142 p.77 Q24050 p.78 HU83790 p.79 Q48451 p.95 Q79836 p.102 Q15064B p.113 Q106364 p.115 Q33161

Mary Greens Picture Library: p.20

BPK: p.39

Hulton Getty: P. 120, 121, 122

'My Boy Jack' by Rudyard Kipling by permission of A. P. Watt Ltd on behalf of The National Trust for Places of Historical Interest or Natural Beauty.

WORLD WAR I
WAR IN THE AIR

PETER HEPPLEWHITE

Six fantastic true stories about war in the air during World War I.

In August 1914 the tiny Royal Flying Corps is flying on reconnaissance trips. Pilots spot a huge German battalion heading their way. But will the generals believe them in time to save lives?

On 10 May 1915 Louis Strange is hanging from his plane by his fingertips – 8,000 feet in the air. How did his obsession with machine guns lead to this? And can he get out of it?

In 1915 German airships roam the skies over England. Are they really invulnerable to attack by aeroplanes or can they be stopped? One man – Reginald Warneford – is going to try.

In 1917 giant German bombers raid London and kill innocent civilians. Will the shock of these terror raids force the British to surrender or can the plucky RFC retaliate?

New pilot Mick Mannock seems boastful yet edgy. If he can overcome his flight nerves he has all the makings of a top-scoring Ace. Will he be able to do it?

With the end of the war in sight, Canadian Ace William Barker is caught alone in the middle of a 60-plane German flying Squadron. How can he possibly make it back home?

A WORLD IN FLAMES

WAR AT SEA

PETER HEPPLEWHITE

Six fantastic true stories about war at sea during World War II.

On 5 November 1940 Convoy HX 84 is attacked by the German battleship *Admiral Scheer*. Can the liner *Jervis Bay* buy enough time to save the convoy?

A week later in the Mediterranean, the Fleet Air Arm attacks Italian battleships in Taranto harbour. Will 21 dated Swordfish dive-bombers be up to the job?

The fearsome battleship, the *Bismarck*, slips out of the Baltic in May 1941. Can the Royal Navy catch her before she escapes to ravage British convoys?

Convoy OB 318 is attacked by the German submarine *U-110*. The escorts fight back. Can they go a step further and capture her precious code books?

In August 1942 Canadian troops lead an assault on the town of Dieppe. It goes horribly wrong. Can the Navy get its men home?

In the autumn of 1943, as cold winds begin to bite in the Arctic circle, the X-craft strike. But will they be able to cripple the battleship *Tirpitz*?

**A selected list of titles available from
Macmillan Children's Books**

The prices shown below are correct at the time of going to
press. However, Macmillan Publishers reserve the right to
show new retail prices on covers which may differ from
those previously advertised.

Peter Hepplewhite		
World War 1: In the Air	0 330 41011 3	£4.99
World in Flames: Sea	0 330 48295 5	£4.99
Maneaters	0 330 48357 9	£3.99
Sandy Ransford		
Alien Puzzles	0 330 39220 4	£2.99
Puppy Puzzles	0 330 37512 1	£2.99
Holiday Jokes	0 330 39771 0	£3.99
A Puzzle for Every Day	0 330 48486 9	£4.99
Secret Agent's Handbook	0 330 39915 2	£3.99
Philip Ardagh		
WOW!	0 330 40049 5	£4.99

All Pan Macmillan titles can be ordered from our website,
www.panmacmillan.com, or from your local bookshop
or are available by post from:

**Bookpost
PO Box 29, Douglas, Isle of Man IM99 1BQ**

Credit cards accepted. For details:
Telephone: 01624 836000
Fax: 01624 670923
E-mail: bookshop@enterprise.net
www.bookpost.co.uk

Free postage and packing in the UK.

Contents

About the author

Professor Greg Wilkinson
graduated in medicine at
Edinburgh University and trained
as a psychiatrist at the Maudsley
Hospital in London. He is
Professor of Liaison Psychiatry at
the University of Liverpool, where
he has responsibility for teaching
medical students and undertaking
research on mental health
problems.

Coping with stress

What causes stress?
What does cause stress? Anything that makes you tense, angry, frustrated or unhappy. It may be thinking about next week's driving test or a visit from a difficult relative; the choices you have to make when moving house or getting married; the seemingly unrelenting

pressures of work; or the unavoidable burden of coping with a death in the family.

Factors that stress some people give others excitement. Racing drivers and mountaineers seem to thrive on physical challenges. Some people enjoy the excitement of going to sea in bad weather and join the lifeboat crew. Others choose to work on high buildings and rooftops. So, one person's stress may be another person's pleasure.

In fact, a certain amount of stress is good for us. When we have to face up to a challenge or we are made to get on with some job that we don't want to do, we often find that we can achieve the targets that we have been set. We then feel a lot better having done it. Facing challenges and overcoming them stops us from getting bored. In fact, many people deliberately create mild stress in their lives to overcome periods of dull routine.

How does stress affect your body?

Stress sets off wide-ranging changes in the chemical control (neurotransmission) of the body's hormone system called the hypothalamic–pituitary–adreno-cortical system (known as the 'HPA axis' for short).

The first part of this system, the hypothalamus, controls the pituitary gland in our brain, which activates the adrenal glands in our abdomens. For example, in acute stress, discharge into the blood of adrenal stress hormones, such as adrenaline (now called epinephrine), leads to the 'fight or flight' response, with increases in startle, anxiety, heart rate, blood pressure and blood glucose, sweating or flushing, decreased appetite, disturbed sleep and decreased sexual activity.

Adrenaline and the fear response

Adrenaline (epinephrine) is released in the body in response to a physical threat or opportunity. It has a variety of effects within the body to ensure that we are ready to deal with the situation.

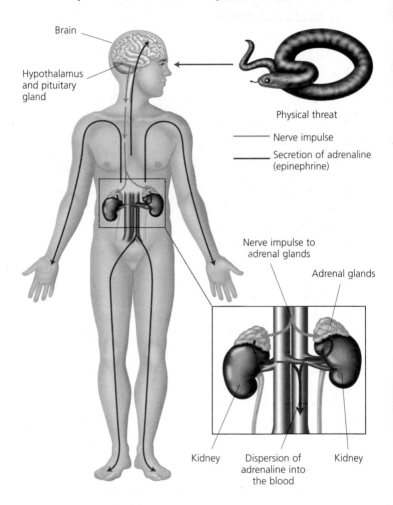

Brain

Hypothalamus and pituitary gland

Physical threat

——— Nerve impulse

——— Secretion of adrenaline (epinephrine)

Nerve impulse to adrenal glands

Adrenal glands

Kidney

Dispersion of adrenaline into the blood

Kidney

The parts of the brain called the hippocampus and amygdala bring together information from our environment and from our memory, allowing us to assess the significance of a stressful situation, and driving the hypothalamus to increase output of the hormone cortisol from the adrenal glands during stress.

In chronic stress, the altered stress hormone release contributes to undermining health (for example, causing depression, stomach ulcers, decreased immune function perhaps with susceptibility to viral infections, heart disease, and disturbing the symptoms or treatment of many other medical conditions).

In particular, repeated stress beginning in early life leads to over-responsiveness of the pituitary and adrenal systems, and eventually to chronically raised hormone secretion at levels that may have consequences for different bodily organs and vulnerable areas within the central nervous system.

Too much stress

Too much stress, however, affects our health and well-being, and may interfere with our jobs and our social lives. Repeated, continuing, severe stress has a weakening and demoralising effect, which may make it more difficult to do anything about the factors that are causing the stress.

Just how we respond to pressure is determined by our characters, and by our personal disabilities or illnesses. These dictate how we react to difficulties with relationships, both at home and at work, and to practical problems over money, work and housing.

How we respond to pressure is influenced also by our external environment (for example, what individual and group social support is available to us). This in turn

influences how we react to difficulties with relationships: with family at home, colleagues at work and friends in our leisure time. This then plays a part in affecting how we respond to social and community pressures (for example, shaping one way or another our view of our body and ourselves, drinking and drug use, and spiritual and sexual behaviour).

A question of adjustment

As we grow and mature we become better at knowing what to expect in our everyday life, and what to do about the things that upset us. We become better at dealing with the unexpected. We learn to make adjustments in attitude, and the way that we behave, in order to understand and to cope. Usually this is fairly straightforward and we are hardly aware that we are 'coping with stress'.

When events of major importance take place, however, such as marriage, birth or the death of someone close, our reactions and the way that we cope are more obvious to us.

In order to live successfully with stress, we need to spend some time considering the sources of stress in our lives and whether our physical and emotional responses to these are sensible and useful, or are preventing us from coping and taking control.

Although studies show that the ability to cope with stress is partly inborn, it is also a question of training, upbringing and practice.

A survey by the Health and Safety Executive has shown that half a million Britons suffer illnesses related to stress at work, and this is probably an underestimate.

Overcoming stress

There is every reason to be optimistic that you will be able to overcome the stress in your life. There are several simple and effective methods that can be used to reduce and overcome stress and, in most cases, these self-help solutions are very successful.

Although almost everyone is under some form of stress, only a few ever respond by developing a physical or emotional illness that requires specialist help.

KEY POINTS

■ Stress is caused by anything that makes you tense, angry, frustrated or unhappy

■ One person's stress may be someone else's enjoyment

■ A certain level of stress is good for us

■ Too much stress affects our health and well-being

■ There is every reason to be optimistic that you will be able to overcome the stress in your life

■ Stress sets off wide-ranging changes in the chemical control (neurotransmission) of the body's hypothalamic–pituitary–adrenocortical (HPA) hormone system.

Balancing coping and stress

I have already said that stress can be both a good thing – a motivator – and a bad thing. Furthermore, what is stressful may not only vary from one person to another, but can change for one individual from year to year.

This is because the way that stress affects us depends on a balance between the demand made by the event(s) causing the stress and our ability to cope (which can vary considerably). Too large an imbalance between demand and ability to cope may result in the sort of stress that is not good for us.

Looked at in a slightly different way, the overall level of stress depends on a complicated balance that takes account of the stressful event, our response to this in terms of physical effects, cognitions (for example, memory, awareness and decision-making), emotions and outward behaviour, and how significant the event is to us (is it something that makes us very happy, deeply sad or is it not too important?).

How stress adds up

Stress level	= Potentially stressful event(s)	+ Our response to the event(s) (physical, emotional, cognitive or behavioural)	+ Significance of the event(s) to us (happy, sad, worried or indifferent)

For example, if John Smith, with a large mortgage, a wife, three children and a job that he enjoys and is important to him, is made redundant, he is put under a great deal of stress. The event is of major significance to him, and he may suffer physical symptoms (increased heart rate and blood pressure, inability to sleep, eat or relax, and emotional bursts of anger and irritation) which affect his outward behaviour.

When driving, John's cognitions may be decreased at the edges of his vision, and he may not be aware of, or respond quickly enough to, what is happening on the side of the road, leading to an accident or 'near miss'.

Jill Brown, on the other hand, is 23, highly qualified, with no responsibilities and a job that she finds boring. If she is made redundant, she may not be shattered. Instead, she may feel that the event has forced her to make a long overdue change, and she may be relieved and relax, feeling better than she has done in ages. In this case, stress has a positive side and is needed to introduce a necessary element of change in her life.

We can see from this that similar stress events may bring out an entirely different response in different people.

KEY POINTS

■ The way that stress affects us depends on a balance between the demands made and our ability to cope

■ Physical symptoms of stress may sometimes result from an individual's inability to deal with it

Sources of stress

We would all become extremely bored if nothing ever
happened in our lives. However, any major change
needs to be balanced with our ability to cope with that
particular change at the time in question.

Too much change, too quickly, can be a major cause
of stress. The demands are far too much for our ability
to cope. An indication of how much stress various

typical life events and social changes may cause is given in the table on page 15.

In general, the greater the number of these events that happen to us in a given time, such as a year, and the higher their combined rating, the more likely we are to suffer a stress response, either emotional or physical. Moreover, the severity of the stress response is usually related to the significance of the events and changes.

Remember that stress can be triggered by events that are thought of as pleasant, such as getting married, winning money or having a baby, as well as by unpleasant events such as losing a job, having an accident or the illness of someone in the family.

Life events

When evaluating the impact of life events and social changes as a cause of stress, we also need to take into account the fact that life events tend to be particularly stressful when they are:

- unpredictable
- unfamiliar
- major
- intense
- unavoidable
- inevitable.

Do be careful, however, not to take the contents of the table on page 15 too literally. It is common for people who feel stressed to search for the reason in past events, but some life events can be the result, rather than the cause, of the stress. For example, a feeling of not being able to cope with new duties or

responsibilities may be the result of unrecognised stress rather than the stress being the result of a failure to cope with the situation.

So sources of stress lie mainly in these events in our lives and in our physical, cognitive and emotional responses to such events. If you are already under stress and not paying attention at work, your performance may well be affected, leading to disciplinary action. The initial stress-induced cognitive inattention leads to another life event. The cause may be obvious to us, in which case the way we need to react may be straightforward and clear cut, and depend on us making practical or emotional adjustments. In these circumstances, it may be easy to see where we should ask for help.

Often, though, the source of stress is not quite so obvious and it may need some careful thought or talking through with others to bring it out into the open.

Life events and stress

Event   Stress rating

Event	Stress rating
Death of husband or wife Divorce or marital separation Jail term Death of close family member Personal injury or illness Marriage Loss of job Moving house	**Very high**
Marital reconciliation Retirement Serious illness of family member Pregnancy Sex difficulties New child Change of job Money problems Death of close friend	**High**
Family arguments Big mortgage or loan Legal action over debt Change in responsibilities at work Son or daughter leaving home Trouble with in-laws Outstanding personal achievement Partner begins or stops work Start or finish of school Change in living conditions Revision of personal habits Trouble with boss	**Moderate**
Change in work hours or conditions Change in schools Change in recreation Change in church activities Change in social activities Small mortgage or loan Change in sleeping habits Change in contact with family Change in eating habits Holidays Christmas Minor violations of the law	**Low**

Adapted from Holmes and Rahe.

What factors affect you?

To help discover the source of your stress, ask yourself whether there are any social, physical or emotional factors that are affecting you:

- How many tea/coffee/caffeinated drinks are you having?
- How much are you smoking?
- How much alcohol are you drinking?
- Are you taking enough exercise?
- Could you be ill?
- Is there some new element in your life?
- Has there been any change in your general circumstances?
- Have long-standing problems recently become worse?
- Is someone close to you facing difficulties that affect you?

Again, unrecognised illness may affect our ability to cope, or there may be difficulties with relationships that we are not prepared to face.

Sometimes, however, we may never find an answer and very occasionally stress does come 'out of the blue'.

Life phases

You may get a clue about stress levels from considering the phase of life that you are in. In the late teens, many major decisions have to be made for the first time. In mid-life, responsibilities are often heaviest and most dramatic. In old age, there may be illness, deaths in the family and money problems to cope with on your own.

You should also consider the phases of life that those close to you are in. Crying babies, bedtime blues, little monsters, know-it-alls, getting to school, teenage rebels – no parent gets it right every time. Even family mealtimes can be the most stressful occasions in everyday life.

Conflicts in your life

Ask yourself whether there is anything that you would like to sort out. For example:

- Do you have continual disagreements about someone or about something?
- Is some situation leaving you with a feeling that you are not good enough, or that it is all your fault?

- Are you taking, or being made to take, a new or unaccustomed role – or are you perhaps carrying, or being asked to carry, too much responsibility?

- Do you have unspoken fears or frustrations about your life?

Often stress is the result of a build-up of related and unrelated factors of these kinds. If you settle down quietly and list the stresses in your life, you may be surprised – and relieved – to discover that some of the stresses are ones that you can eliminate.

The warning signs of stress

The warning signs that stress may be affecting your health vary considerably from person to person. The signs may be visible or 'invisible' and have short- or long-term effects. Most of us, however, have our own usual stress response or 'fingerprint'.

This might be headaches in one person, or an outbreak of eczema or diarrhoea in another. The signs may be less obvious (for example, poorer control of an existing medical condition). Usually the first signs of stress are changes in our emotional life or behaviour, and at times the differences can become more noticeable to others than they are to us.

Emotional reactions to stress

The most important changes to watch out for are increases in tension, irritability and moodiness. Small irritations may seem unbearable if they come on top of stress, and can cause a major outburst or upset. For example, the fact that the children want to play a board game when you have just come home from work, and you simply want to sit down and relax, may make you feel that you want to put them up for adoption; or you may find that you have an

overwhelming desire to perpetrate grievous bodily harm on your car when it refuses to start; and when the toaster will not pop up your slice of toast you have to be held back from attacking it with the bread knife.

There may also be changes in appetite or weight: some people lose interest in food, whereas others have a constant desire to eat. Your ability to cope at home and at work may become extremely variable: you may find that you can't quite get round to paying the household bills, and are spurred into action only when the phone has been disconnected; and your brain seems to have moved into reverse gear at work so that the 'in tray' gets bigger and bigger. You smoke or drink (or both) more, which does, however, help fill in the time in the evening as you seem to have difficulty in sleeping.

The box on page 21 gives some examples of different emotional reactions to stress. If you notice some of these signs or other people point them out to you, take

Emotional reactions to stress

- Feeling under pressure
- Feeling tense and unable to relax
- Feeling mentally drained
- Being constantly frightened
- Increasing irritability and complaining
- Feeling of conflict
- Frustration and aggression
- Restlessness, increasing inability to concentrate, or to complete tasks quickly
- Increased tearfulness
- Become more fussy, gloomy or suspicious
- Being unable to take decisions
- Impulses to run and hide
- Fears of imminent fainting, collapse or death
- Fears of social embarrassment or failure
- Lacking in ability to feel pleasure or enjoyment

notice; unless you take steps to protect yourself, you are at risk of experiencing increasing stress. You may not recognise all the signs at first, however, or you may have overlooked or ignored some for a variety of reasons. You may also have to resist a tendency to regard the reactions as definite evidence of serious physical illness rather than a response to stress.

Physical reactions to stress

Physical reactions to strong emotions were designed to save us in the days when we led the simple, dangerous life of the caveman. To Stone Age man these bodily responses meant fight or flight and prepared him for action; millions of years later they still do – which is very useful if a woolly mammoth is on the rampage, but not a great deal of help when we have just missed the last train or dropped the car keys down a drain in the road! What happens to our body is that our pulse and blood pressure increase, we breathe more rapidly and our ears, eyes and nose become more alert. These changes are the result of the action of stress hormones released into the blood circulation in response to the event (see pages 2–4).

When the stress response goes on for a long time, or occurs frequently and at the wrong time, it may lead to a wide range of unpleasant feelings. The number and nature of physical feelings differ greatly between people, but the most common are listed in the box on page 24.

How to deal with the physical symptoms of stress

The most effective techniques for dealing with physical reactions to stress are controlled deep breathing and relaxation. These are discussed on pages 53–7. It is important to be relaxed regularly throughout the day and not only when you are 'relaxing'.

Try to start noticing bodily sensations and, whenever you feel physical reactions to stress, try to relax your muscles; for example, drop your shoulders, and relax your facial and tummy muscles. If you can, stop what you are doing and rest, spend time quietly calming down, and practise distracting yourself, deep breathing and relaxing your muscles. Start by taking a deep breath and slowing down your breathing. Take a deep breath, hold it in while you count up to three ('one hundred and one, one hundred and two, one hundred and three') and then slowly breathe out.

Repeat this exercise and continue slow, relaxed breathing at around 10 breaths per minute. If you feel

Physical reactions to stress

- Muscle tension
- Rapid, uneven or pounding heartbeat
- Fast, shallow breathing
- Sweating
- Dilated pupils
- Over-alertness
- Change in appetite
- Muscle weakness or trembling
- A sick feeling in the stomach
- Sleep problems
- Jumpiness
- Headaches
- Weakness of the limbs
- Indigestion
- Frequent urge to pass urine
- Chest discomfort
- Odd aches, pains or twitches
- Constipation or diarrhoea
- Tiredness and weakness
- Worsening of long-standing discomforts or pain
- Constant restlessness and fidgeting
- Backache
- 'Pins and needles' in hands or feet
- Dry mouth or throat
- 'Butterflies' in the stomach

comfortable, you can increase to a 'six-second breath', counting one hundred and one through to one hundred and six. (Fast shallow breathing can increase physical reactions to stress.) Then slowly go back to what you were doing or carry on to where you were going – continue to breathe slowly and deeply, distracting yourself, and thinking constructively and positively about how you handled the situation and how you will deal with it should it recur.

Behavioural reactions to stress

The behaviour of people under stress can change quite considerably. Often they hate to be alone and make efforts to seek out support from family and friends. Some may become withdrawn and indifferent. They seem to have lost interest in others and even start to turn down invitations because everything feels as if it will cause too much trouble.

They continually seek reassurance and can become indecisive – a trip to the supermarket for a packet of tea bags seems to require as much thought and preparation as the ascent of Everest. They change their minds a lot and they may speak fondly of someone one moment and find them completely useless the next. They may be tearful, difficult and complaining, and often expect others to be impossibly understanding of them.

There may be a change in sexual habits (a loss of interest, an increase in casual sex or altered sexual

preference), and the previously mild-mannered may become verbally or physically aggressive.

A person who used to be fairly relaxed may become rigid and obsessive, repeatedly checking locks and switches, for example, or cleaning the oven at three in the morning when previously it was done once a year.

Actions of this sort may be due to an effort to bring some order and certainty to the sense of confusion which they feel is surrounding them. Often the person under stress denies these behavioural changes but they are usually very obvious to other people.

Ask friends whether they have noticed any changes in your behaviour, but don't be cross with them for telling the truth – remember that denying the obvious can be a sign of stress!

KEY POINTS

- Too much change too quickly can be a cause of stress

- Stress can be caused by pleasant and unpleasant events

- The cause of stress may not always be apparent

- Usually stress is a result of a build-up of related and unrelated events

- Often your stress is more apparent to others than to yourself

- Reactions to stress can be emotional, physical, cognitive and behavioural

Tackling the problem

Identify stress

The difficult thing about stress is recognising it; doing something about it is relatively easy. Once you have recognised that you are suffering a stress response, you should be able to identify and tackle any underlying

causes, not just the symptoms. And you can ask someone whom you trust and respect to help.

Keep a record of stress

First of all list all your signs of stress, noting how severe they are and for how long they have lasted. Next, list all the possible causes that you can think of and sort them into categories.

Remember that a series of minor irritations may be more distressing than the major problems of life.

Having written down all the possible causes of your stress, you can sort them into those that have a practical solution, those that will get better anyway, given time, and those that you can do nothing to change. You should try to let go of those that fall into the second and third groups – what you cannot change try to stop worrying about. Your teenage daughter may give up her attempts to be a model and go back to college, or she may be so successful she becomes a millionairess. The drilling outside will be a distant memory a month from now.

Where there *are* practical solutions (and this applies to most problems) make a list of these and try them out to see if they improve the situation.

You should be prepared for the fact that some of these solutions may upset people. Remember that looking after yourself does not mean being unkind to others, and that you are most useful to yourself and to others if you are functioning well.

Monitor progress

The next stage is to monitor your stress response by keeping a note or brief diary of the changes in the nature, severity or duration of the signs. After a week,

Sample stress diary

Stress sign	Severity (out of 10)	How long it lasted	Category
Sleeplessness	I often lie awake for hours (9/10)	The last six weeks	Family and friends
Under pressure	I dread going to work in the morning (7/10)	At least three months	
Racing heart	Sometimes I feel faint (5/10)	The last two weeks	
6 weeks later Sleeplessness	Difficulty sleeping (5/10)	Three nights last week	Work
Under pressure	Feel better about going into work if I stop for breakfast in a nearby café (3/10)		
Racing heart	Not too bad last week (1/10)		
12 weeks later Sleeplessness	Better since altered bedtime routine and exercising regularly (1–2/10)		Leisure interests
Under pressure	Got to consider my next career move – is this the right time? (1/10)		Finances
Racing heart	Better with breathing exercises and relaxation tape (1/10)		Health & appearance
			Home environment

Causes of stress and possible solutions

Possible cause of stress	What type of stress?			Possible solutions(s)
	Has a practical solution	Will get better with time	Cannot influence or change	
My mother has had a bad fall			X	You cannot change what has happened; ensure that the family help her
My daughter has dropped out of college		X		She knows her own mind and in time you will accept the situation
I feel that I am being left out	X			The solution is in your hands; get involved in: family, clubs, sport, voluntary work, local politics, education
I am pushing myself too hard	X			There are practical steps that you can take: structure your time, delegate more, give yourself space to think, prioritise activities, have proper breaks during the day, discuss workload with boss/colleagues, reorganise tasks to achieve a balance
Year-end deadlines		X		They will pass and so will your stress
I spend all my spare time watching telly	X			Develop a wider range of interests: arts/crafts, sport, films, concerts, theatre, reading
Credit card account	X			Stop using it or use it only for essentials
I am getting old			X	Accept the situation and grow old gracefully
My husband is taking a long time re-decorating	X			Offer to help, be patient!

repeat the process to see how you are getting on: if some of the solutions do not seem to be working, try alternatives.

Keep assessing progress until you feel that you have reduced as many of the causes of stress as possible and that you are in control of things. Almost certainly things will have vastly improved over 6 to 12 weeks.

Control your lifestyle

Too much to do and too much responsibility? To avoid feeling overwhelmed you can divide chores into what you 'must' do, what you 'should' do and what you 'need not' do. The following points may help you to feel more in control of your life:

- Plan a daily or a weekly timetable of activities. Try to include something fresh and enjoyable each day.

- Plan for the future and do not dwell on past mistakes or disappointments.

Ways in which you can help yourself

1 Write down your hourly timetable. For each activity score 0 to 10 for the pleasure it gives you and 0 to 10 for how well you carry it out. Keep a check on your progress every few days.

2 Make a list of what you need to do.

3 Plan your timetable to:
- do things that need to be done
- do things that give you more pleasure
- do things that you can do well.

4 Concentrate on goals that are achievable all at once or in small steps.

5 Check for unhelpful patterns of thinking, such as: 'I can't cope with this'; 'I've got to get out of this'. How true are these thoughts? Are there other ways of thinking about the situation?

6 Write down the problem(s) and all the possible options for change and then try them out, beginning with the most achievable.

- Cut down on smoking, alcohol, caffeinated drinks; exercise regularly; eat proper meals; get enough sleep.

- Find time for rest and relaxation.

- Involve your family and friends in helping to change your lifestyle.

Unhelpful thoughts
Change your thinking

To change the way that you think, you need to do the following:

- Think about your thinking. Reward your successes and challenge your criticisms.

- Look out for and record unhelpful thoughts that pop into your mind without any effort on your part, that do not fit the facts, that you don't question and that are difficult to switch off. Write down as much as possible to begin with. Fast, effective responses will become easier with practice.

- Learn to recognise unhelpful ways of thinking and substitute more realistic and helpful thoughts. By regular practice this will become easier. Start off by writing your thoughts down until you get the hang of it.

- Resist the temptation to avoid thinking about unhelpful thoughts but beware of making excuses – ignoring the problem will not make it go away.

- Record as many unhelpful thoughts and your responses to them as possible each day. You may need to work out 50–100 responses to unhelpful thoughts before you can do it in your head. Write down as much as possible to begin with. Effective responses will become easier with practice.

In particular, you need to consider four aspects of persistent unhelpful thoughts.

For instance, if you feel that your new work colleagues do not like you:

1 Q How do the thoughts relate to the facts?
A *My colleagues all acknowledge me and smile.*

2 Q What are the alternative interpretations?
A *Everybody is very busy, nobody has time to relate to anyone else particularly.*

3 Q What are the pros and cons of thinking this way?
A *These thoughts may affect how I am projecting myself to my workmates.*

4 Q Are you jumping to conclusions or blaming yourself unnecessarily?

Recognise unhelpful thoughts

Count up how many unhelpful thoughts you have each day and how much of the time was taken up with these thoughts. For example, you might feel that you have to put up with a shoddy repair job at home because you feel that you wouldn't know what to say if you tried to complain. Or that a meeting went badly at work because you are not up to your job.

Over several days you may begin to see a pattern emerging.

If something leads to more unhelpful thoughts – AVOID IT

If something leads to fewer unhelpful thoughts – DO MORE OF IT

Use unhelpful thoughts as a cue for action. Write them down as they occur in a daily diary.

Analyse your thinking

Thinking about thinking is not something that we usually do and you may find it difficult at first. It is difficult to think of different options when you feel stressed.

Just write down what is troubling you and return to it when you feel more at ease. There is no right answer; look for solutions that help you to be more positive.

When every movement seems an effort, the best response can be to make yourself do more.

Benefit from activities

Any activity is positive, because it:

- Makes you feel better: it distracts you and gives you a sense of control over your life, achievement and pleasure.

- Gives you the strength and stamina to feel less tired.

- Helps you become motivated: the more you do the more you want to do.

Twenty questions to help you deal with unhelpful thoughts

1 Is it a thought or is it a fact?

2 Jumping to conclusions?

3 What is the alternative?

4 What is the effect on me of thinking this way?

5 What are the advantages and disadvantages?

6 Is there any answer to this? (What is the meaning of life?)

7 Am I thinking in black and white terms?

8 Are the issues really as clear cut as 'always versus never' and 'everything versus nothing'?

9 Is everything wrong because of one event or change?

10 Are my weaknesses over-shadowing my strengths?

11 How appropriate is blame?

12 How much of this is to do with me?

13 How perfect can I be?

14 Have I got double standards?

15 Is there only a down side?

16 Is everything likely to be a disaster?

17 Are things out of proportion?

18 Am I living life the way it is or the way that I'd wish it to be?

19 Isn't there anything that can change?

20 What can I do to affect the outcome?

- Helps you think straight.
- Pleases those around you.

Make an activity schedule

An activity schedule gives you information about what you are doing now and what more you can do in the future. It confirms that you are not 'doing nothing'.

For three days record exactly what you do hour by hour. Give each activity a rating between 0 and 10 for enjoyment (E), pleasure (P), achievement (A) and mastery (M), with 10 being the most rewarding and 0 the least.

E10 means that the activity was highly enjoyable and A10 means that there was a high sense of achievement.

Make the ratings at the time of the activity and not in retrospect, and relate them to you as you are now and not to how you once were at some perfect time in the past.

Plan activities

What would you like to improve? How can you change things for the better?

Plan each day in advance, including activities that give you enjoyment and a sense of achievement.

- Structuring time allows you to feel that you are gaining control and have a sense of purpose.
- A daily or weekly framework provides meaningful structure for living.
- Once the day's or the week's activities are planned and structured, they are broken down into a series of manageable units that are less overwhelming.

Sample problems and possible solutions

Write down all the problems that you experience during the course of the day. Then list ways in which you can combat or solve the problems.

Problems	Solutions
✗ I can't cope with having the in-laws to lunch.	✓ If I write down what I need to do it won't be so overwhelming. I can take the things one at a time. I don't have to do them all at once.
✗ It's too difficult to sort out the muddle at work.	✓ I've done more difficult things than this in the past.
✗ I don't want to go to an exercise class.	✓ I don't now but I did earlier on. It would be better for me to do it. I'll feel good about it afterwards.
✗ I don't think I'm up to making a difficult phone call just now.	✓ I won't know until I try. If I wait till I feel like it I'll never do it. I'll feel better when I've done it.
✗ I won't be able to do everything I've planned because there simply isn't enough time.	✓ No one does all they've planned. Think about what I have done, not what I haven't.
✗ I can't decide which thing to do first because they're all equally important.	✓ Do the first in alphabetical order. The most important thing is to do something. Once I get started I'll have a clearer idea of what to do next.

Make the most of activities

- Be flexible, not a slave to routine.

- Think of alternatives – you can't picnic when it rains.

- Keep to the plan. If you have some 'free time', fill it in with something from a list of pleasurable activities that you keep handy.

- Schedule activities by the half hour or hour.

- Concentrate on how much time you are going to spend, not how much you are going to do in the time available. You weed for an hour, not to collect a hundred-weight of weeds!

- Work to the schedule. Work steadily to gain results.

- Review the situation. What have you enjoyed achieving?

Getting started

Try combating your problems in the following way:

- Make a list of things that you have been putting off, such as getting the car serviced, phoning an awkward relative.

- Number tasks in order of priority and try to do those with the highest priority. For example, if your car is making odd noises and hasn't been near a garage for months, that job should be near the top of your list.

- Break the first task into small steps:

  Check your diary to see whether you'll be needing the car for something vital

  Find the garage phone number. Ring and book it in.

- When you face a difficult task, rehearse the task in your mind step by step. You will have prepared and planned what to do and what to say, and thought of and gone through options to deal with possible complications.

Write it down

Write down difficulties that you foresee and how to get round them.

- Stop when you are doing well and you will feel good about what you have achieved and ready to try again.
- When you finish, immediately write down what you have done on your activity schedule and rate it for enjoyment and achievement.
- Concentrate on achievements.

Remember next time

- Go back and look at your priority list again.
- Tackle the next task in the same way.

KEY POINTS

■ Once you have recognised that you are suffering a stress response, then you should be able to identify and tackle any underlying causes

■ List your signs of stress

■ List the probable causes of your stress

■ Monitor the changes in the nature, severity or duration of the signs of your stress

■ Look out for unhelpful thoughts and think of new solutions to them

■ Try your solutions out

■ Plans and activities are powerful weapons to overcome stress

Defences against stress

We can defend ourselves against stress in our lives by understanding what causes us stress, and by learning how to avoid or adjust and adapt better. The principal defences are within ourselves, and mainly consist of physical and mental fitness – a healthy body and a healthy mind.

Physical defences

We can improve our defences by leading a healthy, enjoyable life and by looking after ourselves.

Sleep

First, we should ensure that we get enough sleep and this can be helped by learning how to relax (see pages 53–7). As Macbeth says in Shakespeare's play, sleep 'knits up the ravell'd sleave of care'. The amount needed varies from person to person, but it is probably true to say that more is needed during times of stress than when life is running quietly and smoothly. Beware, however, of taking too much sleep – it can make you feel almost as bad as too little. Sleeping problems are very common among those under stress, but do make sure that you do not worry unnecessarily about a few bad nights – you can usually catch up after one good night's sleep.

If you are having difficulty in sleeping, reduce your overall daily consumption of tea, coffee and soft drinks containing caffeine; eat supper early and avoid strong tea or coffee, unless it is decaffeinated, in the afternoon and evening.

Try to tire yourself physically by taking some pleasant exercise, for example, a brisk walk or gardening, have a bath and then spend some time switching your mind off before going to bed by reading or watching television or even playing 'patience'.

Do not allow yourself to brood over problems; they can wait until the morning! If you can't get to sleep, or wake in the middle of the night and can't get to sleep again, get up, make yourself a drink (preferably with hot milk, and not tea or coffee), have another game of 'patience' or do some mindless chore like sorting your sock drawer out or tidying the tool box, and then go back to bed. Do not lie in bed worrying.

Try not to take sleeping pills unless it's only for one or two nights in order to break the pattern of sleeplessness. They can make you feel fuzzy and dopey in the morning, and can develop into an unwelcome habit which could end up causing even more stress.

Food and nutrition

Try to keep to the ideal weight for your height. We should all eat a sensible diet to avoid the health hazards of being overweight, and to reduce or prevent the risks of developing diseases known to be related to diet, such as heart disease, high blood pressure, bowel cancer and late-onset diabetes. Currently obesity rates have been increasing, and diet and dieting ('yo-yo dieting') may be the cause and effect of stress. Whereas this section advocates the benefits of healthy eating, professional help or structured support with diet may be required at times because self-help approaches to dieting can induce weight gain unless highly structured.

The main principles are to eat far less fat and fatty foods, especially those containing saturated fats and cholesterol; increase dietary fibre by eating more whole-grain cereals, pulses and fresh fruit and vegetables; cut down on sugar and salt. This can be difficult as it goes against all that many of us hold dear, such as the

What should you weigh?

- The body mass index (BMI) is a useful measure of healthy weight
- Find out your height in metres and weight in kilograms
- Calculate your BMI like this

$$BMI = \frac{\text{Your weight (kg)}}{[\text{Your height (metres)} \times \text{Your height (metres)}]}$$

e.g. $24.8 = \dfrac{70}{[1.68 \times 1.68]}$

- You are recommended to try to maintain a BMI in the range 20–25
- The chart below is an easier way of estimating your BMI. Read off your height and your weight. The point where the lines cross in the chart indicates your range of BMI

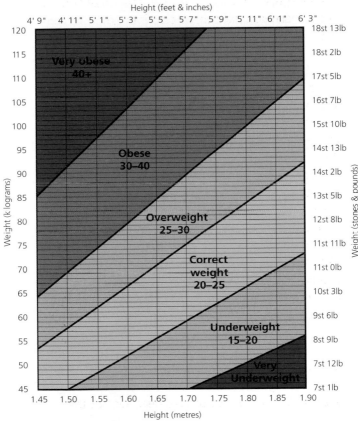

traditional Sunday lunch of roast beef, Yorkshire pudding and roast potatoes!

Don't go too quickly in your campaign for diet reform; change a few products at a time and add new foods rather than just cutting out those that you currently eat and are bad for you. If you live for Sunday roast lunch, don't abandon it completely. Just try to cut back on the fatty bits. Changing your diet should not be a torture – it should be fun!

Be careful about what you drink. Too much tea or coffee can be over-stimulating and excessive alcohol is certainly no friend to good health. You should also avoid drinks with a lot of sugar or caffeine.

Physical activity

There is only one way to keep the body trim and fit. We all need some regular physical activity, preferably daily. This might amount to no more than a pleasant, brisk 20-minute walk in the fresh air, but it could well be much more. At the very least, you will be more likely to feel physically and mentally relaxed, be able to get a refreshing sleep and your appetite will be stimulated. There are also some health benefits, such as illness prevention, lower heart rate and blood pressure, improved well-being and mood, and social benefits (for example, making new friends). The important thing is that the physical activity chosen should be pleasurable – which for some of us is a problem!

Helping yourself with activity

Whatever you decide to do in the way of exercise, always bear the following points in mind:

- Warm up for two or three minutes before starting by stretching or running on the spot.
- Build up slowly and do not over-extend yourself – always exercise within the limits of comfort (let your breathing be your guide) and, if it hurts, stop.
- If you feel excessively tired, stop and rest – there is always tomorrow.
- When stopping activity, cool down gradually and slowly to avoid stiffness.
- Activity sessions three times a week for about 20 minutes, at a pace that keeps you moderately 'puffed' (not gasping for breath), are likely to be best for stimulating both muscles and circulation.

Mental defences

Improving general health and fitness can protect against and lessen the effects of stress. Some events are in themselves stressful, but many of our reactions to these depend on our attitudes, beliefs and values. The mind has a whole series of defence mechanisms, described in the previous chapter of this book, and although these may be helpful in the short term, they may act as a barrier to adapting and coping with stress.

In overcoming stress we often do not have appropriate or enough coping strategies available. We need to learn new skills of self-instruction and self-control.

Social defences

Social support, from spouse or partner, someone close, family, neighbours, a group or a community, can act as a protective buffer against the effect of stress. Other forms of social support such as having a confidant(e), avoiding isolation, exchanging information on coping strategies, advice and practical help – such as for finances – and social or leisure activities are also excellent defences against stress. For example, people who are bereaved do better with good social support than those without. However, too much social support – for example, over-involvement – may be as damaging as too little. And, obviously, the way in which people seek help has a bearing on how supportively others respond.

Self-instruction

When we learn a new skill, such as driving a car, we learn from a combination of observation and instruction. At the beginning, we are usually instructed by someone else; then we repeat the process, giving the instructions to ourselves; finally, once we have learned the skills, we are able to drive 'automatically' without consciously thinking of what we are doing.

We can apply a similar process of:

- observation
- instruction
- self-instruction
- automatic ability

to our everyday thinking.

For example, suppose that we feel stressed about taking examinations or having job interviews. First, using a little imagination before the event, we can pay attention to the way that our thoughts tend to work when the stress is imminent. What are the things that we say to ourselves? Perhaps 'Oh, my God, what can I say?'; 'I wish this was all over'; 'I wish I hadn't started this'; 'Two hours still to go'; 'They must think I'm an idiot'; and so on.

Next, we can make a list of positive, practical instructions that would be more useful. Such as 'I had better start writing' rather than 'I'm very nervous'; or 'These are the main points and these are things I want to emphasise' rather than 'I don't know what they're looking for'.

Third, during the event, we instruct ourselves positively with the most useful instructions that we have thought of beforehand, instead of wasting time and energy panicking or ruminating on irrelevant thoughts. In time this process becomes 'automatic'.

Self-control

Having a sense of control over events lessens their stressful impact. True, there are some things over which we have no control, but there is usually some aspect of a problem that we can change to our advantage, thereby reducing stressful feelings of helplessness.

Self-control methods can be very useful when we wish to alter particular aspects of our behaviour or response to people or events.

First, carefully observe the behaviour in question, for example, always getting angry with Bloggins at work, or being irritable with the family at breakfast time, or regularly missing the bus/train because you leave home

with too little time to spare. Chart the circumstances in a diary made up for the purpose.

Now, think of practical ways in which you can modify the behaviour. For example, take a deep breath and ask Bloggins if you can help him. Make a point of saying something nice at breakfast. Make sure you leave home in plenty of time to catch the bus/train.

The next part of the process of self-control involves reward. Choose something pleasant with which to reward yourself when you change the behaviour in question and reach a certain predetermined standard – buy yourself a treat if you manage to catch your bus/train every morning for a whole week without rushing!

Relaxation

Relaxation is a useful technique to practise when you feel under stress, and can lead to reduced anxiety and physiological changes – for example, decreased muscle tension and reduction of blood pressure, while relaxing – and help to promote sleep when practised at bed-time.

There are a number of similar methods, but one of the most widely used is described on pages 56–7. Read the instructions and familiarise yourself with them before having a go. You may be able to borrow a 'relaxation tape' from your general practice or local library. Do be patient, and give yourself several tries before expecting the full beneficial results – for those of us who are very 'twitchy' it can take time to learn to relax.

To begin with practise for 30 minutes three or four times a day, then slowly reduce the 'dose' to once a day as you feel better. If you feel under stress again, increase the dose!

The advantages of regular relaxation

- Improves sleep

- Increases mental and physical performance

- Combats tiredness

- Decreases anxiety and tension

- Is not addictive.

Preparing for relaxation

Before starting on any relaxation routine, it is important to ensure that your mind, body and environment are properly prepared. The following steps are a guide to such preparation:

- Sit in a comfortable chair or (even better) lie down somewhere comfortable in a quiet, warm room where you will not be interrupted.

- If you are sitting, take off your shoes, uncross your legs and rest your arms on the arms of the chair.

- If you are lying down, lie on your back with your arms at your side. If necessary use a comfortable pillow for your head.

- Close your eyes and be aware of your body. Notice how you are breathing and where the muscular tensions are. Make sure that you are comfortable.

Breathing to relax

In order to relax it is essential that you use the correct breathing technique. Follow the steps below to improve your breathing technique:

- Drop your jaw and shoulders.

- Breathe slowly and deeply, in through your nose and out through your mouth, expanding your abdomen as you breathe in, then raising your rib cage to let more air in, until your lungs are filled right to the top.

- Hold your breath for three to six seconds and then breathe out slowly, allowing your rib cage and stomach to relax, and empty your lungs completely.

- Do not strain – with practice it will become much easier.

- Keep this slow, deep, rhythmic breathing going throughout your relaxation session.

- Remember to breathe deeply and be aware when you relax of the feeling of physical well-being and heaviness spreading through your body.

Putting it all together

Bring together the stress management techniques for day-to-day use through a combination of the monitoring of physical and mental signs of stress, use of self-instruction, deep breathing and relaxation as a means of rapid stress control.

For example, stick a red dot at the centre of your watch as a regular reminder to practise monitoring physical tension and any thoughts that might be causing stress during the day.

Practise challenging thoughts (tell yourself 'stop getting worked up') or, at a minimum, ease yourself into relaxing by saying 'relax' and do this by taking a slow, deep breath, holding it for three to six seconds and letting it out slowly while practising your relaxation technique at the same time.

Relaxing

Once you have established a breathing pattern (after five to ten minutes following the instructions on pages 54–5), start the following sequence, tensing each part of the body as you breathe in, holding your breath for ten seconds while you keep your muscles tense, then relaxing and breathing out slowly at the same time.

To estimate ten seconds, you should say 'one hundred and one', 'one hundred and two', etc.

Relaxation sequence

1 Curl your toes hard and press your feet down.

2 Press your heels down and bend your feet up.

3 Tense your calf muscles.

4 Tense your thigh muscles, straightening your knees and making your legs stiff.

5 Make your buttocks tight.

6 Tense your stomach as if to receive a punch.

7 Bend your elbows and tense the muscles of your arms.

8 Hunch your shoulders and press your head back into the cushion or pillow.

9 Clench your jaws, frown and screw up your eyes really tight.

10 Tense all your muscles together.

11 After ten seconds, relax.

12 Close your eyes.

13 After you have done the whole sequence (1–11) and, while still breathing slowly and deeply, imagine a white rose on a black background. Try to 'see' the rose as clearly as possible, concentrating

Relaxing (contd)

your attention on it for 30 seconds. Do not hold your breath during this time; continue to breathe as you have been doing.

14 Repeat step 13, visualising another peaceful object of your own choice.

15 Lastly give yourself the instruction that, when you open your eyes, you will be perfectly relaxed and alert.

16 Open your eyes.

17 Repeat steps 1–16 five to ten times.

Once familiar with this technique, you can use it even if you just have a few minutes by leaving out some muscle groups – but always work from the feet upwards.
For example, you may do steps 1, 4, 6, 8 and 10.

KEY POINTS

- We can defend against stress by understanding what causes it

- The principal defences against stress are physical and mental fitness

- Physical, mental and social fitness are improved by healthy lifestyle, adequate sleep, eating a balanced diet and taking regular physical activity

- Our mental fitness to deal with stress is helped by self-instruction and self-control

- Relaxation techniques are useful when you feel under stress

How to help yourself

Many people find their own ways of tackling stress without the help of doctors or other health professionals.

The main questions to ask yourself are:

- 'Is there anything I can do when I feel stressed that makes me feel better?' If so, keep doing it (alcohol and 'false friends' excepted).
- 'Is there anything I do that makes me feel worse?' In general, avoid it if you can.
- 'Is there anything that I think might help if only I could do it?' Try it out if at all possible.

Tackling problems

In addition to looking after yourself, a problem-solving approach can help you to find exactly what the stress is and devise a plan to cope with it. Even though some stresses cannot be fully resolved in this way, you will usually find that you're more able to cope, so that the overall impact of stress is reduced.

Rejecting unpleasant thoughts

Miserable feelings and unpleasant thoughts tend to focus your attention on things that you do not like about yourself or your life. They tend to exaggerate problems so that they seem overwhelming and make you feel worse.

Although it may be difficult to distract yourself from unpleasant thoughts, it does help to decide not to think about them and fill your mind with something else. You can do this by a combination of:

- concentrating on events around you such as other conversations, the number of blue things you can see, in fact anything that holds your attention
- any absorbing mental activity that you enjoy, such as mental arithmetic, games, puzzles, crosswords and reading

- any physical activity that keeps you occupied, such as going for a walk, doing housework or taking a trip.

Strategies to help you reject unpleasant thoughts

Unpleasant thoughts make you tend to underestimate your positive characteristics and ability to solve problems. A number of strategies may help you achieve a more balanced view of things. Recruit a friend or relative to help you see things more clearly:

- Make a list of your three best attributes, perhaps with the help of a friend or relative. Perhaps people would describe you, for example, as generous, affectionate and reliable.

- Carry the list with you and read it to yourself three times whenever you find yourself thinking unpleasant thoughts.

- Keep a daily diary of all the small pleasant events that happen and talk about them with a friend each day.

- Recall pleasant occasions in the past and plan pleasant ones for the future, again with a friend if possible.

- Avoid talking about your unpleasant feelings – expressing unreasonable thoughts about yourself is unhelpful; tackling your real problems is more constructive.

- Ask friends to interrupt such negative conversations politely and focus instead on more positive ideas.

- Always consider alternative explanations for unpleasant events or thoughts rather than automatically blaming yourself.

- Keep your mind occupied by planning and doing constructive tasks – avoid sitting or lying around daydreaming or doing nothing.

Physical symptoms of stress

Stress is almost always accompanied by symptoms of anxiety, tension, worry or nervousness, such as muscle tension, trembling, cold sweats, butterflies in the stomach, rapid or difficult shallow breathing, and a rapid or irregular pounding heartbeat. This response may be triggered by situations such as an enclosed space, a crowded supermarket or even meeting a friend.

At other times unpleasant thoughts, for example, of dying or possible failure in work, may trigger these feelings of anxiety and panic.

Why the panic?

It's almost always possible to identify situations or thoughts that trigger this panicky feeling. Remember that anxiety is not harmful and always goes away after a time.

- Wait and the feelings will pass.
- Practise one of the plans on pages 63–5. Use it whenever you feel panicky.

- It can be helpful to start by taking a deep breath and then slowing down and deepening your breathing pattern.

- Try to distract yourself by concentrating on something pleasant as this will stop you adding to the panic.

- As the panicky feeling subsides plan something pleasant to do next.

Plans that help put worry behind you

Worry is a pretty pointless activity and never solved anything, so here are three plans to counter it.

1. Problem solving

Put your worrying to constructive use. Rather than endlessly pin-pointing your problems, pick out one or two that seem really important and make specific plans to resolve them (you may find it helpful to do this with a friend). Sit down with a sheet of paper and pencil and go through the following steps making notes as you go:

- Write down exactly what the problem is.

- List five or six possible solutions to the problem – write down any ideas that occur to you, not merely 'good' ideas.

- Weigh up the good and bad points of each idea in turn.

- Choose the solution that best fits your needs.

- Plan exactly the steps that you would take to achieve the solution.

- Reassess your efforts after attempting to carry out your plan (remember to praise all your efforts).

- If you are *unsuccessful* start again – this time trying a new plan.

2. Rethinking an unpleasant experience

- List every feature of the experience: 'I'm sweating . . . the hairs on my arm are standing on end . . . my heart is pounding hard . . . I think I'm going to start screaming . . . my legs feel like jelly . . . I'm going to pass out'. Write these down on a card.

- Talk yourself into staying with these unpleasant feelings. Tell yourself exactly how you feel and remind yourself that the feelings will reach a peak and then get better.

- Re-label your experiences: imagine you are playing an energetic sport – a cup final, singles finals at Wimbledon – and that this accounts for your pounding heart, rapid breathing and feelings of excitement.

- Think catastrophic thoughts, focusing your mind on the worst possible thing that could happen to you, for example, collapsing, screaming, throwing your clothes off, being sick or incontinent, etc.

- Plan exactly what you would do if it did actually happen. Next time it will be a little easier to cope with the feelings and with practice and monitoring you will find that you are beginning to control and overcome worry.

3. Relaxation exercises (see pages 53–7)

Take an interest . . .

- Set some goals for your daily activities: for example, I will get up by 9am, meet a friend, read an article in the newspaper.

- In *small steps*, build a full programme of constructive activities for the day.

- Avoid comparing your current levels of performance and interests with those in the past – concentrate on the here and now and on the future.

- *If a task* seems too difficult do not despair. Break it down into even easier steps and start again more slowly.

- Above all reward yourself for your efforts.

- Try to have others around you to encourage and praise you for every small step that you take.

Dealing with specific stress symptoms
Loss of appetite

It may be more a case of fluctuations in appetite, and not necessarily just loss of appetite. Cortisol (a stress hormone) stimulates fat and carbohydrate breakdown for fast energy, and stimulates insulin release and maintenance of blood sugar levels. The end result of these actions is an increase in appetite. Therefore, during times of stress it is possible to see both an increase and a decrease in appetite control.

- Eat small portions of food that you particularly like.

- Take your time eating.

- Temporarily avoid situations that make you feel under pressure to finish eating.

- Drink plenty of fluids, especially water and fruit juices.

- Weight loss may be an important indicator of the extent of stress so if you continue to lose weight seek help from your GP.

Loss of sexual drive

Decreased interest in sex is frequently a feature of stress and is a cause of much distress.

It won't last forever, but, in the meantime, try to enjoy those aspects of your sexual relationship that are still a pleasure. You can explain to your partner that your loss of interest and affection is a temporary symptom of your condition not a rejection of him or her.

If your interest shows no sign of reviving within a few weeks, discuss the problems with your GP or another professional adviser or confidant(e). Things can improve with help.

Setbacks

Everyone has setbacks from day to day. These are to be expected and you should try to keep your mind on your long-term goals. To counter feelings of disappointment a setback should be thought of as just moving down one rung of the ladder, rather than going straight to the bottom. You might find it helpful to:

- approach the problem in a different way

- approach the difficulty in smaller steps or stages

- continue practising because eventually this will help you overcome your difficulties

- remember that you will probably be more successful if you can make your activities or rewards as enjoyable as possible.

Ask friends to help

It is common to think that you are not making any progress to begin with and to underrate your achievements. It's a good idea to have a member of the family or a friend to give you an independent opinion about your progress and to offer encouragement.

Keep a stress diary

A simple daily or weekly record or diary will help you keep track of improvement. The first signs are usually quite small, sometimes hardly noticeable, but writing everything down will help you see exactly what has happened. Don't just rely on your memory: people have a tendency to remember setbacks more than

successes. Again it is helpful to involve someone else in assessing your improvement to give an independent opinion.

Keeping a stress diary

A stress diary is an important part of helping to deal with stress. Work through the following steps:

- Write down what happened
- Score yourself from 0 to 10 (best) for each day or week
- Write down all your successes, large or small
- Write down what self-help technique you were using, what target you were trying to achieve and whether you were practising it regularly
- Write down what you did not avoid thinking about or doing
- Write down what you did for enjoyment or fun
- Look back at your diary every week to see what progress you have made and to make plans for what you intend to achieve next week

KEY POINTS

■ Many people find their own ways of tackling stress

■ Anxiety always goes away after a time

■ Worry is a pointless activity and never solved anything

■ Confront your problems and make plans to solve them

■ Everybody has setbacks – and they can be overcome

Getting help

Talking to friends and relatives

Coping with stress can be made easier by having some support and help from family and friends. In fact, not having any family or friends to call on may itself create or worsen stress.

For example, if you are feeling anxious or uncertain about something that has recently happened, such as getting into debt or worrying that you might be going to lose your job, your stress may be increased by not having anyone to whom you can tell your fears.

You may easily believe that other people don't worry in the same way, that there is no way you can escape from the pressure and that no one else is interested. You could be convinced that no one else understands or has experienced similar anxieties about such a common event, and that the fact that you are having difficulty in coping is a sign of weakness and something to be ashamed of and hidden.

Good friends and loving relationships help to counteract stress. Support can be found in having a stable home life or a trouble-free atmosphere at work. Such a refuge can provide breathing space, enabling us to work our way through and sort out a particularly stressful problem for ourselves.

It is an enormous help if you have someone to talk to who will listen sympathetically and in confidence and who will, if you want, provide moral support, practical advice or company, or simply be there to take your mind off your problems.

Talking to someone helps you to see a problem more clearly, to get things in proportion, to explore all the possible answers and to face up to, and learn to get through, the causes of your stress.

Feeling alone

Many people, unfortunately, do not (or think that they do not) have any close family or good friends to turn to for help. Loneliness and isolation may be difficult to escape from; fear of rejection may put you off trying

to make new friends. But the important thing is to recognise the need for outside help, and not to see this as a failure and something to be ashamed of. If you already have a large family and/or a social network of friends, then you will need to learn how to benefit from them in coping with stress.

If, on the other hand, feelings of isolation are a major part of the problem, you could try to develop a social network by offering friendship and support to others and receiving it from them in return. You will benefit from making the effort to find new friends and stimulation through, for example, classes, courses, sports, voluntary work or political activities.

None of these steps is easy, and all involve making a conscious effort to look outward, to be open and receptive to others, and optimistic and resilient in the face of difficulties, but they can, in time, be extremely beneficial and rewarding. Try not to forget that there are other people feeling just as isolated and with just

as much potential for giving, as yourself: to find them you must come out of yourself.

Who can help you cope with stress?

If you are not coping with stress, get help as soon as possible – the earlier help starts the better. You may find that the very act of seeking help and discussing problems with your family and friends gives immediate relief.

Professional help

There are three main types of professional help available: medical, psychological and social. In practice these elements are often combined in the various treatment packages offered by different professionals – except that prescriptions for medication can be written only by medical doctors.

GPs, social workers, clinical psychologists, community psychiatric nurses, counsellors and psychiatrists have important roles to play. The personal qualities of such people are important and should include acceptance, warmth, genuineness, empathy, a tolerant attitude, dependability, continuity and an interest that allows them to take even seemingly minor problems seriously.

The traditional medical approach to treatment has been criticised for being too narrow and neglecting personal and social aspects. As a result of this criticism a variety of psychological approaches has been developed for use in addition to medical treatment or alone.

Your GP

For many people under stress, particularly those with no or few confidant(e)s, the family doctor becomes the first and chief source of help. Doctors deal with all aspects of life that affect health but, like other people, they vary in their reaction to the stress responses with which they have to help.

Most GPs prefer to deal with stress by counselling and general advice. Even the act of giving a full account of the circumstances surrounding the stress,

with the doctor listening carefully to the descriptions, is usually beneficial because it helps to get the stress in perspective, so that adjustments and decisions can be made.

The doctor may perform a thorough examination and, in a few cases, arrange for special blood tests. The signs of stress may seem overwhelming to you and appear to mean disease, and it is reassuring to find out that no serious disease is present and that the body is functioning perfectly efficiently, even under stress.

Whatever the outcome, an appointment with the GP is a good opportunity to discuss alternative ways of reducing stress as well as where help and further information can be obtained.

Mental health services within the NHS

For most people the first professional contact is their GP. Often access to specialist help from psychiatrists, clinical psychologists, psychotherapists and others in the NHS can be obtained only through your GP. Occasionally specialists will agree to see you without a GP referral, but they usually want to keep your GP aware of their involvement. If you want to see a specialist but for some reason cannot get a referral, it is worth getting in touch with your local hospital to find out if you can be seen by self-referral.

Mental health services, like other services within the NHS, are under severe pressure. Most people are treated by their GP and if they are referred to a hospital specialist it can take some time before they are seen.

Private specialists

You can see a psychiatrist or other mental health specialist privately. This can be arranged by your GP or by getting in touch with a local private psychiatric hospital or clinic.

Self-referral

As a result of pressure on hospital services and criticism of the traditional medical approach, there are an increasing number of voluntary and private self-referral agencies. Details are usually available from your local community health council, Citizens Advice Bureau, social services department, library or community centre.

If, as well as loneliness and isolation, some more serious or specific difficulty is involved, then the various caring agencies can also provide support on a temporary or long-term basis. There are, in addition, a number of national organisations that offer help, advice and information about particular conditions or problems, and they will usually be able to give you further details about local facilities.

Notice boards in local libraries are often a good source of information about local helping agencies and facilities. Your library should have access to a copy of the Mental Health Foundation's *Someone to Talk To* directory or a similar guide, which lists all these groups.

The essential thing is to try to identify the source of stress in your life, decide what kind of help you think would be best for you and seek help from the people or agencies that you feel most comfortable about approaching. Also, try to recognise that, like you, the people you turn to will have different strengths and weaknesses, and if you feel that a particular approach is not working, say so, and see if it can be changed or (preferably by mutual agreement) try elsewhere.

Do not be deterred if your first approach does not bring an instant solution – keep trying.

Voluntary bodies

Voluntary bodies such as The Samaritans can provide a sympathetic ear, information and advice. Your local health authorities will have a health information service and contact numbers for local voluntary groups. Where relationship problems are important, it may be useful to contact your local branch of Relate. See 'Useful addresses' on pages 122–141.

Ministers of religion

For many stressed people there is a natural tendency to turn to religion for spiritual solace and support. For those who believe, the strength of shared belief and the sense of belonging and common purpose can overcome adversity and demoralisation. Ministers of religion usually have great experience in counselling and are often more than willing to talk things over and provide support.

Support and counselling

GPs and most health professionals often find themselves in the position of giving emotional support, advice and counselling in an effort to provide reassurance, encouragement and sympathy.

Indeed this is probably the most common and most successful help. In many cases, listening may be more important than giving advice – provided that listening means not only hearing the words spoken but also taking note of what the person is saying and trying to understand how she or he feels.

- Your counsellor should allow you to express appropriate emotions and reassure you that they are perfectly 'normal'; a hand on the shoulder may do more good than any number of words.

- Any irrational anger and guilt that you feel are accepted and not discounted.

- You can talk through your feelings, events leading up to a crisis.

- You can test the reality of events described.

- You can explore the implications.

- You may find encouragement to seek new directions in life.

But beware of seeing problems as entirely the result of stress and beware of becoming dependent on professional helpers.

What is counselling?

Counselling is the name given to a range of activities in which an attempt is made to understand the effects of some event on an individual or family, and to plan, with the person or people concerned, how to manage the emotional and practical realities. The purpose is not to impose an answer, but to assist the person to live the life that he or she has consciously chosen.

As almost anyone can set up as a counsellor, it is wise to ensure beforehand that the person whom you choose is trained, qualified and experienced. You can do this by asking for advice from your doctor or one of the self-help agencies.

Also, a list of qualified counsellors can be obtained by sending a self-addressed envelope to the British Association for Counselling and Psychotherapy (see page 126).

There are many different counselling techniques, but the main characteristics of a successful counsellor are emotional warmth, understanding and genuineness. You also need to feel that he or she is someone to whom you can relate. Counselling usually takes place regularly over a period of weeks or a few months.

Reassurance
This is still probably the most widely used form of counselling. Bland reassurance is seldom, if ever, useful, but careful listening will help identify the main stress, and then reassurance can consist of 'new' information that is relevant to reducing the stress, put in a form that is easy to understand and remember.

Behavioural counselling
Behavioural counselling aims to change behaviour. The main concern is to relieve a specific difficulty or symptom by studying the patterns of behaviour that led to difficulty, and then modifying responses by

learning more useful ways of dealing with problems. The emphasis is on 'doing' rather than just 'talking'.

People who have difficulties with relationships (for example, shyness or embarrassment) can learn useful new 'social skills' in this way. After discussing and observing your behaviour, the counsellor or therapist may first explain the effects of this on other people, perhaps using a videotape to show you how you function.

When you have together identified the problems in your approach, the therapist may then coach you in new, more effective ways of behaving, and get you to act them out in a 'role play' with other people. Alternatively, the therapist may ask you to take on the role of someone with whom you have particular difficulties, to help you see more clearly and from a different angle how your own responses work.

Rational–emotive counselling

Rational–emotive counselling considers the way in which we 'worry about being worried'. It involves identifying the irrational ways in which we think about problems, and then helps us find less stress-provoking ways of dealing with them.

Rogerian counselling

This type of counselling (based on the work of Carl Rogers) is not based on telling us what to do, but on

helping us work out for ourselves what we want and how best to achieve it. The counsellor's job is to facilitate self-understanding by 'mirroring back' to us our own understanding, to help us to re-shape our thoughts and feelings, to share our experiences and to discuss their development with us.

Humanistic counselling

This is concerned with 'personal growth', and helping us to achieve our full potential. Workers in this form of counselling make use of encounter groups and personal therapy, massage, meditation, dancing, co-counselling and virtually any method that seems likely to help people under stress to understand themselves more clearly and to feel better. The main aim of this technique is to integrate the health and well-being of the person as a whole.

Psychotherapy

Any treatment that does not use drugs or other physical

methods could be called psychotherapy. The most important element is talking and it is the ideas behind the therapy, the way it is applied and the nature of the relationships that develop between the person and the therapist which differentiate the various types of psychotherapy.

Some schools of therapy emphasise the importance of loss (of loved ones, objects or cherished ideas); others propose that we humans have an inborn tendency to seek attachments with others that build emotional and social bonds and lead to experiences of warmth, nurture and protection. Destruction of these bonds may make people vulnerable to stress.

The concept of attachment bonds provides a basis for understanding development of personality and for developing strategies to correct distortions produced by faulty or inadequate attachments in childhood.

Strong attachment bonds seem to be especially important and valuable when people are faced with adversity and stress.

Depending on the approach taken by the psychotherapist you may be helped to express and redirect anger and hostility in more appropriate ways, or you may work together to examine current personal relationships, and to understand how they have developed from experiences with attachment figures in childhood, adolescence and adulthood.

Psychotherapy and relationships

The psychotherapeutic approach to treatment has arisen out of various theories that view disturbances in personal relationships as contributing to stress and depression. Particularly important are relationship difficulties such as:

- loss or bereavement
- disputes about roles (specially the roles of husband and wife)
- role transitions (becoming a mother, divorce)
- lack of close, confiding relationships.

In essence, psychotherapeutic treatment is concerned with identifying problems in your closest relationships and in considering alternative ways of behaving and thinking.

The discussion between the person and the therapist concentrates on:

- emotions generated by close relationships (including warmth, anger, trust, envy, jealousy)
- family relationships
- friendship patterns
- work

- attitudes to neighbourhood and community.

What are the shortfalls of psychotherapy?

Many people assume that one or other variety of psychotherapy would suit them. Psychotherapy, especially psychoanalysis, which may last years, is often prolonged, intensive and expensive. In addition it is not easily available throughout the country. It is very difficult to judge its benefits, whether it's given individually or in groups. For these reasons, and because it is possible for some people to feel worse and more stressed after psychotherapy, this treatment is generally considered inappropriate for most people.

Changing your thinking

Your therapist may help you choose actions that are likely to change unhelpful ways of thinking – 'learning from experience'. It is not enough simply to help you change the content of a particular thought; it is essential that you should recognise and change the reasoning process that led you to a false conclusion, if you are to avoid making similar errors in the future.

Although the 'cognitive' therapist pays particular attention to the intrusive unhelpful thoughts that precede the change of mood or feeling of stress, he or she is also concerned to question the deeper assumptions that someone makes about the world, because deeper assumptions give power to unhelpful intrusive thought patterns.

First phase

The first task is to help you become aware of any unhelpful thinking and to recognise the relationship between it and emotional states. This can be done by

helping you to recognise unhelpful thoughts during treatment when the stressful episode can be relived using role play.

Second phase

The second task is to help you to develop different ways of interpreting events. For example, you may be encouraged to stand back from a problem in order to get a more objective view of it. Different ideas may be sought and you may be asked to rate their correctness.

Once you are able to think of alternative ways of interpreting events you may be asked to keep a daily record of stressful feelings and the thoughts associated with them. You may be asked to reason with your intrusive unhelpful thoughts and suggest other possible interpretations to yourself as soon as a stressful feeling becomes apparent.

Problem-solving

If you are faced with a problem the following steps may help you solve it:

- Define the problem
- Divide it into manageable parts
- Provide alternative solutions
- Select the best solution
- Implement the possible solutions and examine the result

Third phase

The third phase of the process is to encourage you to test out the beliefs and attitudes associated with stressful feelings in a systematic way. Instead of treating ideas as fact, you will be helped to see that it is possible to discover the degree of truth or otherwise of your beliefs through enquiry.

As you improve and learn the cognitive approach, the focus of treatment moves to deeper assumptions which are thought to underlie unhelpful thinking patterns. Unless these are identified and modified you are likely to become stressed again in the future. As these beliefs have usually been present from an early age, they tend to be resistant to change. There are no simple ways of highlighting these faulty assumptions, but a useful start is for you to identify recurring stress themes in your life. The best way to break the pattern is to encourage you to act against these deep assumptions.

Approximately 15 sessions over three months are needed for most people requiring this specialist treatment. Two sessions a week are usually held in the first month followed by weekly meetings thereafter.

Social approaches for dealing with stress

These cover all efforts to improve a patient's well-being by changing aspects of his or her social life, particularly in regard to family relationships, bringing up children, work and leisure activities. Of course, defined in this way virtually all treatment consists of some social elements – even visiting the GP is a social event.

At the most simple level, having a holiday, taking time off work and taking up a new interest are all important social means of trying to relieve stress. Education, sport, music, art, nature, science and religion all offer great opportunities for social encounters that can improve well-being.

Also, for example, SureStart (see 'Useful addresses', page 139) is a recent government programme designed to deliver the best start in life for every child, bringing together early education, childcare, health and family support. Services are for children from conception to age 14, and up to age 21 for those with special educational needs and disabilities. It also aims to help parents and communities across the country.

Family therapy

More complicated forms of treatment also contain a strong social ingredient. Family approaches to treatment, sometimes called family therapy, treat the person in relation to the family. This does not mean that the family is held responsible for the individual's stress, but many of the problems of stress can revolve around difficulties in the way family members communicate and relate to each other. Bringing the family together for group discussions is sometimes a powerful way of helping everyone 'pull together instead of apart', of improving communication and of helping parents develop better relationships with their children and vice versa.

Group therapy

Through discussing problems in a group over a period of a few weeks or months, this type of therapy helps combat social isolation, reminding people with stress that they are not alone, and provides the opportunity for mutual encouragement and discussion of practical ways of overcoming stress.

Art therapy, play therapy, dance therapy, movement therapy, drama therapy, music therapy and gymnastics can all help people develop new social skills as well as practise old ones, increasing self-confidence and self-sufficiency. All aim to provide enjoyment, diversion, stimulation and increased self-esteem and achievement in a social context.

Types of therapy available

There are several different types of therapy available to stress sufferers. The following list of the most commonly used therapies also details some of the benefits of each.

Supportive psychotherapy
- Aims to provide regular reassurance and encouragement.
- Sessions are informal and take place less frequently than formal psychotherapy – perhaps once a month.

Counselling
- Aims to help you help yourself by understanding why you feel the way that you do and planning how to cope with emotional and practical realities.
- Helps you to live the life that you have chosen by discussing current problems and alternative practical solutions.
- Provides a considerable amount of social support over several weeks or months.

Psychotherapy
- Talking is the main tool of treatment, and the different schools encourage talking about different aspects of your condition.
- Sessions usually take place weekly over a period of six to nine months.

Behavioural therapy
- Believes that behaviour is 'learned' and can therefore be 'unlearned' or changed.
- Aims to stop you behaving in unhelpful or unwanted ways and to learn new patterns of behaviour that will make your life more enjoyable.
- Concentrates on how you behave at present and not on theories about why you learned to behave in certain ways. Usually lasts several months.

Cognitive therapy
(also known as cognitive–behavioural therapy)
- Based on the theory that changes in our emotions and behaviour are determined by our thoughts about events that occur. If we always take a gloomy or frightened view

Types of therapy available (contd)

of life, we will interpret everything that happens in a negative way.

- Aims to help you recognise and change unhelpful and gloomy ways of thinking.
- Incorporates some parts of behaviour therapy. The average course is 12–20 sessions.

Family therapy

- Views you as a member of a family or similar social group.
- Is concerned with how the members of the family or group communicate with each other and with their relationships.
- Aims to resolve distress and conflict without apportioning blame by using various psychotherapeutic methods over a period of months.

Group therapy

- This comprises a group of people, who did not know each other before, coming together with a therapist to help each other with their problems.
- Groups may be made up of people with the same problem or different problems, and they may be single sex or mixed.
- Group members can see that they are not alone in having problems and can get a great deal of support from other members of the group. Usually lasts some months.

Psychoanalysis

- Believes that our behaviour and mental state originate in early experiences in childhood.
- Different schools of psychoanalysis interpret the meaning of what you say differently.
- A great deal of time is spent discussing the relationship between you and the therapist – this is taken to represent the relationship between you and important people in your early life such as your mother or father.
- Psychotherapy sessions take place several times a week over a period of years and so the treatment can be costly in terms of both time and money.

Which treatment is best?

The best treatment is the one that works for you.
All methods have been found helpful by some people
and, if one does not seem to be working after a fair
trial, you should try another until you find some relief
from your stress. The variety of psychological and social
therapies can be quite confusing so I have listed the
main ones (see pages 90–1).

Other ways to relieve stress
Self-help groups

These are groups of people who have a common problem and have joined together to do something about it.
They are small, voluntary groups providing mutual aid
working together towards the accomplishment of some
aim, and provide members with the following help:

- People with stressful problems can feel lonely,
  confused and isolated, and it can help to talk about
  these problems with others 'in the same boat'.

- Support may be given individually or in a group. It may be aimed at helping the individual to adjust to a situation or to take steps to change it. It may be offered in crises or may be available over a longer term.

- Self-help groups provide a wealth of information to help people cope more easily.

- Some forms of help needed to cope with particular problems can be provided directly by mutual aid organisations. These may be provided on a casual or informal basis (for example, baby-sitting), or they may be provided more formally (established playgroups). They may be carried out by group members on a voluntary basis or they may involve hired staff. A few groups even provide services jointly with their local authority.

- Many self-help groups consider that the benefits and services provided by the State are inadequate and so they form a pressure group to bring about favourable changes.

The media and telephone/internet

Newspapers, books, magazines, television, radio and the internet aim to entertain, inform and instruct. Although they are usually passive forms of communication (they do not respond), when used selectively they may be useful in providing practical information about a wide range of interests, and give temporary relief from stress by diverting attention from worries.

The telephone/internet gives confidential access to an enormous number of counselling organisations nation- and worldwide. The most notable source of confidential telephone contact is The Samaritans. Its 24-hour telephone service is provided in the main by

part-time volunteers of all ages and from all walks of life, who have training but whose main strength lies in their willingness to listen sympathetically.

Time – the great healer

Perhaps the most neglected treatment of all is time. Mild stress can get better on its own, given time, and spontaneous improvement over 6 to 12 weeks is the norm. Quite a lot of people do get better anyway, sometimes in spite of the treatment prescribed! Spontaneous natural improvement is most likely, however:

- in a first episode of stress
- when the stress started recently
- where the stress started suddenly
- when relatives and friends can give practical and emotional support.

KEY POINTS

■ Family and friends can provide valuable support in dealing with stress

■ If you are worried about stress, the earlier you tackle it and help begins the better

■ There are three main types of professional help available: medical, psychological and social

■ Give a treatment a fair chance to help you before trying something else

■ Self-help groups and the media can provide a wealth of information, advice and practical help

'False friends'

Bad habits

Smoking tobacco, drinking excess alcohol and taking drugs of dependence (sometimes even sleeping tablets, benzodiazepines or tranquillisers prescribed by the doctor, if not carefully monitored) make stress worse; they are habits that are unwise and should be stopped

or severely curtailed. They are false friends because they provide the illusion of temporary relief, making the processes of defence and successful adaptation much more difficult.

People under stress sometimes attempt to cope, either deliberately or unconsciously, by using these substances to deal with the symptoms that they are experiencing or to withstand the pressure that they feel under.

Alcohol

Alcohol in moderation may be a pleasure, but it is a potentially addictive drug with many subtle and complicated effects. Any long-standing stressful situation invites the serious risk of heavy drinking and eventual dependence on alcohol, which can wreck marriages, family and social life, careers and health (and, of course, you should never drive after drinking).

A unit of alcohol is

| A small glass of sherry or fortified wine | A standard glass of wine | ½ pint of beer or cider ¼ pint of strong lager | A single measure of aperitif or spirit |

A bottle of spirits – brandy, whisky or gin – contains about 30 units

A 'unit' of alcohol may be defined as the equivalent of half a pint of beer or cider (of normal strength), a single measure of sherry, Martini, etc., a single measure of spirits or a small glass of wine. The average man or woman will react to units of alcohol as shown in the tipple table on page 99, with women affected at lower 'doses' than men, the effects being increased by factors such as lack of food, tiredness and stress – and rapid consumption.

Dependence on alcohol

The increasing signs that you may be developing a dependence on alcohol are:

- Awareness of a compulsion to drink.
- Developing a daily drinking pattern.
- Drinking takes priority over other activities.
- Your tolerance for alcohol changes – this usually increases at first but eventually falls.
- Repeated symptoms of alcohol withdrawal – nausea, headache, nervousness, shaking, sweating, tenseness, jitteriness, being 'on edge'.
- Relief or avoidance of withdrawal symptoms by further drinking.
- Rapid return of the features of dependence after a period of abstinence.

Not all these signs may be present, and any one may occur to variable degrees in different people.

'Safe drinking'

Safe levels of drinking are difficult to define precisely for each person, and depend on factors such as gender, body size and constitution. The levels are lower for women than for men.

What is a sensible limit? A unit of alcohol is as described earlier, and medical advice is that the limit for men should be no more than 21 units a week and, for women, up to 14 units a week (if pregnant, alchohol should probably be avoided). In both cases, the units should be spread throughout the week, with two or three drink-free days.

How much is too much? For men, 36 units or more in a week, and for women 22 units or more in

Tipple table

Number of small glasses of wine

Units	Glasses	Effects
1–2		Feeling good and relaxed, but reaction time noticeably reduced
2–4		Some loss of inhibition with poor judgement. Accidents become more likely
3–5		Noticeable loss of inhibition, with physical clumsiness. Beyond the legal limit for driving
4–7		Loss of physical control. Obviously drunk with extreme reactions. Above this level there is progressive loss of consciousness by degrees

Note: women are affected at lower doses than men. The orange glasses denote the numbers of glasses for women, the orange + red for men.

Tips to help cut down drinking

When attempting to cut down your alcohol consumption you may find it helpful to follow the advice below, particularly during the first few weeks:

- Reduce the overall amount by stopping drinking at certain times, for example, lunch time, and do something else instead.
- Keep busy, plan activities that will keep your mind off drink.
- Avoid reminders of drinking and, whenever possible, places where alcohol will be consumed or people who offer you a drink.
- Plan avoidance action for times when you are confronted by these particular situations.

- Drink a long soft drink to quench your thirst before starting on alcohol.
- Allow yourself only one alcoholic drink an hour at any drinking session.
- Add mixers to wines and spirits to increase the volume and so help slow down consumption.
- Avoid drinking in 'rounds' if you are likely to break the above rules.

a week. It is worth remembering that, on average, it takes one hour for the body to get rid of the alcohol in one unit.

Remember that what others choose to drink is irrelevant to your health. Try to find some non-alcoholic alternative in drinking situations.

A man who drinks eight or more units a day (56 a week), or a woman who drinks more than five units a day (35 a week) is at great risk of developing an alcohol-related problem.

You may find it useful to involve a supportive relative or friend who can put up a united resistance with you.

Smoking

The most common reason that cigarette smokers give for not stopping smoking is stress, but cutting out (or certainly cutting down) smoking should be the number one health priority. Tell a smoker that his habit is killing him, however, and the first thing he will probably decide to do is light a cigarette!

The most important step in giving up is the decision that you really do want to stop. Tell yourself the benefits that cessation brings: longer life, better health, more money to spend, clean breath, no cough, fresh smelling clothes, improved ability to taste food flavours, no more standing around outside back doors and street corners in the wind and rain.

Nicotine replacement therapy

Once you make that decision you are halfway there and, if you feel you need some help, it may be worth considering some form of nicotine replacement therapy (NRT): anything from nicotine gum to nicotine patches, the latter being worn on the skin for either 12- or 24-hour periods (depending on which kind you opt for).

Both work by allowing the body to adjust gradually to lower amounts of nicotine. The gum is available on prescription, although the patches can be bought from the chemist – the pharmacist will be able to advise you on the type of NRT that is most appropriate for you.

Questions to help you give up smoking

Initially, forget the 'sensible' reasons for stopping and ask yourself:

- What is smoking doing for me?
- Do I actually enjoy it?
- Do I really need to go through life spending a fortune just to stick these things in my mouth and make myself ill?

However, it's worth remembering that all these replacements are aids, not cures.

Why is it so hard to stop smoking?

Unfortunately, the reasons for stopping smoking actually make it harder to stop. First, because they create a feeling of sacrifice (being forced to give up a little friend, prop, pleasure or however the smoker views cigarettes) and, second, because they create a bind – we do not smoke for the reasons that we should stop – which prevents us from asking ourselves the real reasons for wanting or needing to smoke.

Remember that you had no need to smoke before you became hooked. The first cigarette probably tasted awful, and you had to work quite hard to become addicted. The most annoying part is that non-smokers do not seem to be missing out on anything; in fact, smokers keep smoking to achieve the same state of 'tranquillity' as non-smokers.

So why do you smoke? Forget about stress, boredom and all the other reasons that you may think you have; there are two real reasons – nicotine addiction and brain-washing.

Nicotine addiction

Nicotine is one of the fastest-acting addictive drugs known to humankind. The concentration in the bloodstream falls quickly, however, to about half, in some 30 minutes after finishing a cigarette and to only a quarter within an hour.

The withdrawal pangs from nicotine are so subtle that most smokers do not even realise that they are drug addicts. Fortunately, it is a relatively easy drug to 'kick' once you have accepted that this is the case.

There is no physical pain, just an empty, restless feeling, the feeling of something missing.

If withdrawal is prolonged, the smoker becomes nervous, insecure, agitated, lacking in confidence and irritable. Within seconds of lighting a cigarette, nicotine is supplied, resulting in the feeling of relaxation and confidence that the cigarette gives.

As soon as this cigarette is put out, the chain starts again. The difficulty is that it is when you are not smoking that you suffer the feelings, and you do not, therefore, blame the cigarette. When you light up you get relief and are fooled into believing that the cigarette is the cure for the bad feelings.

So we smoke to feed the little monster, but we decide when to do it and we do it more in stressful situations, when we need to concentrate, when we are bored and when we wish to relax.

Six steps to giving up smoking

Once you have made up your mind to stop smoking, you have to be very determined to succeed. Follow these steps and you will find that giving up is not as difficult as you feared:

1 You decide that you really want to do it, and realise that you can achieve your goal. Remember that smokers are not weak-willed and that it is only indecision that makes giving up more difficult.

2 Recognise and think about the fact that you are addicted to nicotine, but remember that withdrawal is not as painful as you think it is going to be, and that it takes only about 3 weeks to rid the body of 99 per cent of the nicotine.

3 Look forward to the freedom. Do not be afraid of losing the prop you have been brain-washed into believing you need. Smoking enslaves you, preventing you from achieving the peace and confidence that you used to have as a non-smoker.

4 Stop smoking completely. Remember that there is no such thing as just one cigarette – smoking is a drug addiction and a chain reaction. By moping about the one cigarette, you will be punishing yourself needlessly.

5 Watch out for smokers – they may feel threatened by the fact that you have given up, and may try to tempt you back. Try to steer clear of places (especially pubs) that may tempt you to smoke. Drinking alcohol can make you less inhibited, lessen your self-control and increase your risk of smoking again.

6 Keep reminding yourself that there is nothing to give up. On the contrary, there are enormous positive gains to be made by not smoking.

Brain-washing

Nicotine addiction is not the only problem and it is relatively easy to cope with (the smoker does not, for instance, wake up through the night craving a cigarette).

Another major difficulty is 'brain-washing'. The unconscious is a very powerful element in our minds and, despite a whole host of anti-smoking campaigns, we are still bombarded with extremely clever advertising which tells us that cigarettes relax us and give us confidence, and that the most precious thing on earth is a cigarette. Once addicted to nicotine, the power of the advertising is increased, which simply enforces the fear of giving up.

KEY POINTS

- Smoking, drinking alcohol and taking drugs of dependence are not a cure for stress – they all make stress, and coping with stress, worse

- While drinking alcohol in moderation can be a pleasure, heavy drinking carries serious risks to health and well-being – personal, family and at work

- Stress is the most common reason smokers give for not stopping smoking

- Nicotine is one of the fastest-acting addictive drugs known

- Smoking not only ruins your health, it also ruins your finances

Pills, potions and complementary methods

We are experiencing an increasing national dependence on drugs, pills and painkillers of all kinds. We are in danger of reaching the point where we believe that

every ache, pain or worry must be soothed away by taking some kind of treatment, encouraging the idea that any form of stress is harmful. There is a strong link between an overtly pill-conscious society and one that includes a growing number of people dependent on drugs. Some varieties of sleeping tablets and tranquillisers show this connection by the pleasurable effects that they induce in vulnerable people. Experiencing these effects may lead to dependence, and can bring all the complications of dependence on stronger drugs. These complications can include withdrawal symptoms if medication is stopped, and a desperate need to have a good supply in case the drugs are needed.

Many people find complementary therapies of benefit. These include yoga, meditation, autogenic training, biofeedback, the Alexander technique, acupuncture and aromatherapy. Some of these are available at little or no cost, others may prove more expensive (see pages 110–11).

Personal defence mechanisms (unhelpful responses to stress)

Adapting to stress is a two-stage process. First, we have to realise that some of our repeated responses to continuing stress may be unhelpful; second, we need to explore and use new ways of coping until satisfactory solutions are found.

You may sometimes hear social workers, counsellors and psychologists using words such as 'denial' and 'rationalisation' to describe the way people respond to stress. These are technical terms that most people do not come across in everyday speech. I explain them briefly over the next page or so.

Some of these repeated, unhelpful responses – defence mechanisms – are described below.

Complementary therapies

Many complementary methods and treatments are available that can be used to alleviate stress. This table summarises the most easily available and popular methods.

Acupuncture
This is an ancient Chinese medical technique for relieving pain, curing disease and improving general health, and consists of inserting needles into any of hundreds of points located over various 'meridians'. It is a treatment that aims to alter the flow of an individual's bodily energy or life force to relieve pain and restore health.

Alexander technique
This technique teaches people new ways of thinking and using their bodies, with a view to eliminating the effects of unconscious bad habits, such as tension and contorted posture, thereby improving physical and psychological well-being. It is a way of life rather than a therapy.

Aromatherapy
Pure essential oils (obtained from aromatic plants by steam distillation) are used to soothe tension and improve health and mental well-being. The oils are usually massaged into the body, but may also be inhaled, blended or used in baths. Essential oils can temporarily alter our moods and release stress.

Autogenic training
This method of self-hypnosis emphasises individual control over bodily processes through specific exercises. Training usually takes between two and three months, and you learn standard training exercises aimed at inducing a feeling of well-being and coping ability. Specific exercises deal with, for example, breathing, blood

Complementary therapies (contd)

flow and skin temperature. Profound muscular relaxation is achievable.

Biofeedback

Information supplied instantaneously about your bodily processes, for example, blood pressure or heart rate, is monitored electronically and 'fed back' to you by a gauge on a meter, a light or a sound. You learn to detect physical reactions and establish control over them. It can help alleviate symptoms such as pain and muscle tension, and its effects can be lasting if used in combination with counselling to help the person understand reactions to stress.

Meditation

This consists of a number of techniques of concentration and contemplation, which can be effective in controlling pulse and respiratory rates, and in the control of migraine and high blood pressure. Transcendental meditation has been reported to help through reduction of tension, lowering anxiety, and increasing job satisfaction and work performance. Meditators spend two daily 20-minute sessions in a quiet comfortable place, silently repeating their mantra.

Yoga

This is a useful technique for physical and mental relaxation and consists of exercises in physical posture to condition the body. Mastery is reckoned by the ability to hold the postures for an extended period without involuntary movement or physical distractions. Instruction emphasising both the physical and spiritual benefits of yoga techniques is widely available.

Remember, though, that these are only ideas that may help us understand ourselves by showing how our minds work and how we react to stress.

Compensation: developing a behaviour to offset a defect or sense of inferiority – for example, running a pet sanctuary to make up for inadequate human relationships. Thus over-compensation occurs when compensation is overdone.

Conversion: hidden fears may be 'converted' and come to the surface in the form of bodily symptoms. Someone who is afraid of going out may develop a weakness in the legs.

Denial: persuading oneself that there is nothing really wrong when, in fact, there is. This is done in the hope that the trouble will somehow go away – for example, refusing to admit that you are ill.

Displacement: shifting an emotion from one target to another. Ideas or attitudes that make us uncomfortable may be disguised or avoided in this way. For example, anger with our workmates may be taken out on our family.

Dissociation: avoiding looking too closely at our attitudes so that inconsistencies in our thoughts and conduct are overlooked.

Fixation: 'fixed' personal behaviour which is more appropriate to earlier, less mature periods. This is seen in grown adults who depend, child like, on others.

Identification: conscious or unconscious modelling of oneself on another person, which may include the assumption of his or her dress, leisure activities, etc. This may be quite normal: for example, young people often imitate the attitudes and behaviour of older people whom they hold in high regard.

Introjection: the turning inwards on oneself of the feelings and attitudes towards others, which gives rise to conflict and aggression. Unspoken anger with other family members may then lead to self-harm.

Inversion: the exaggeration of tendencies opposite to those that are repressed (see below). Prudery (excessively proper/prim attitude), for example, may be an inversion of repressed sexual desire.

Projection: the opposite of introjection, the displacement of personal attitudes on to others or the environment. This is another way of avoiding self-blame and guilt. Personal inadequacies are blamed on others or even on the environment.

Rationalisation: a form of self-deception in which socially acceptable reasons are found for conduct that is prompted by less worthy motives.

Regression: going back to the ways of thinking, feeling and behaving that are more appropriate to earlier stages of individual or social development. Thus, an adult may regress to childish temper tantrums.

Repression: the pushing out of consciousness of ideas and impulses that do not fit in with what the individual regards as correct in the circumstances. Repression is unconscious and involuntary, in contrast to suppression, which is the intentional refusal to have thoughts or feelings, or carry out actions that conflict with moral standards.

Resistance: a barrier between the unconscious and conscious mind, preventing the resolution of tensions or conflicts. For example, someone might unconsciously resist enquiring into the origins of his stress, thereby prolonging his condition.

Sublimation: the direction of undesirable or forbidden tendencies into more socially acceptable channels. For example, childish, self-indulgent behaviour is sublimated into entertaining or altruistic social behaviour in the process of maturity. Surplus energy may be sublimated into useful channels.

Transference: the experience of emotions towards one person which are derived from experience with another. For example, anxious or hostile feelings previously felt towards a domineering parent may, in later life, be felt in relation to figures of authority.

Withdrawal: giving up, and physical and emotional retirement from a stressful situation, characterised by loss of enthusiasm and interest, apathy and day-dreaming.

Using the golden rules

If you stick to the Golden Rules, on pages 116–17, you will help yourself become calmer and more relaxed. You will have to keep working at it to get the full benefit; work out a practical routine and stick to it, not just for a few days. And remember to enjoy yourself – that is the best cure for stress.

Learn to relax and take things easy for at least an hour each day – a warm bath, taking your time, enjoying pleasant feelings, a relaxing walk or reading

Golden rules for reducing stress

Stress is unhealthy only if you have too much of it. Keep your stress at a manageable level by following these essential tips.

- Get your priorities right – sort out what really matters in your life.

- Think ahead and try to anticipate how to get round difficulties.

- Share your worries with family or friends whenever possible.

- Try to develop a social network or circle of friends.

- Exercise regularly.

- Lead a regular lifestyle.

- Give yourself treats and rewards for positive actions, attitudes and thoughts.

- Get to know yourself better – improve your defences and strengthen your weak points.

- Think realistically about problems and decide to take some appropriate action; if necessary, distract yourself in a pleasant way – don't 'bottle things up' or sit all night brooding.

- Try to keep things in proportion.

- Don't be too hard on yourself.

- Seek medical help if you are worried about your health.

- There are always people who are willing and able to help, whatever the problem – don't be unwilling to benefit from their experience.

Golden rules for reducing stress (contd)

- Relax and take short rests throughout the day, every day.

- Make small, regular changes to your lifestyle.

- Learn to delegate.

- Make space for leisure time.

- Have proper breaks for meals.

- Make time for yourself every day and every week.

- Listen carefully to those around you.

- Enjoy yourself, and your family and friends.

an interesting book can help release you from the things that cause you stress.

Breathe deeply and gently, count to ten, and think again. Take one day at a time – accept a bad day, tomorrow may be better.

KEY POINTS

- Becoming dependent on pills and potions creates further problems

- Many people find alternative therapies such as yoga of benefit

- Overcome stress by understanding and controlling your response to it

- Remember to use the golden rules for reducing stress

Conclusion

Although we cannot, and indeed must not, avoid stress, we can learn to meet it efficiently and live with it successfully, rather than letting stress overwhelm us to the extent that it affects both our mental and physical health.

As a result of the enormous individual differences in the causes of stress, and in our abilities to cope, this book cannot hope to give all the answers to everyone's problems. What I have tried to do, however, is to help you think about, and identify, the undesirable stresses in your own life, and learn how to control these – either alone or with the help of others.

Taking stock of ourselves and our lives from time to time can be an extremely beneficial exercise. It is amazing how little we question our priorities and how many sources of unnecessary stress we can get rid of by doing this.

Useful addresses

Age Concern Cymru
Ty John Pathy, 13–14 Neptune Court, Vanguard Way
Cardiff CF24 5PJ
Tel: 029 2043 1555
Fax: 029 2047 1418
Helpline: 0800 009966
Email: enquiries@accymru.org.uk
Website: www.accymru.org.uk

Actively involved in policy making and raising public
awareness through research. Supports the
development of local Welsh branches and refers to
local groups.

Age Concern England
Astral House, 1268 London Road
London SW16 4ER
Tel: 020 8765 7200
Fax: 020 8765 7211
Helpline: 0800 009966 (7 days a week 7am–7pm)
Email: ace@ace.org.uk

Website: www.ageconcern.org.uk
Order line: 0870 442 2120
Order line fax: 0870 800 0100
Travel insurance: 0845 601 2234

Researches into the needs of older people and is involved in policy making. Publishes many books and useful fact sheets on a wide range of issues from benefits to care, and provides services via local branches.

Age Concern Northern Ireland
3 Lower Crescent
Belfast BT7 1NR
Tel: 028 9024 5729
Fax: 028 9023 5479
Helpline: 028 9032 5055
Email: info@ageconcernni.org
Website: www.ageconcernni.org
Travel insurance: 028 9023 3341

National headquarters in Northern Ireland offering information and advice on a wide range of subjects of interest to people aged 50 or over, including finding and paying for residential and nursing homes. Refers to local branches.

Age Concern Scotland
113 Rose Street
Edinburgh EH2 3DT
Tel: 0131 220 3345
Fax: 0131 220 2779
Helpline: 0800 009966 (7am–7pm 365 days/year)
Email: enquiries@acscot.org.uk

Website: www.ageconcernscotland.org.uk
Travel insurance: 0845 601 2234

Offers information sheets on a range of subjects and a wide variety of services to elderly people through local support groups.

Alcoholics Anonymous (AA)
PO Box 1, Stonebow House
Stonebow, York YO1 7NJ
Tel: 01904 644026
Fax: 01904 629091
Helpline: 0845 769 7555
Website: www.alcoholics-anonymous.org.uk
Northern Ireland branch: 028 9043 4848

Offers information and support, via local groups, to people with alcohol problems who want to stop drinking.

Alzheimer's Society
Gordon House, 10 Greencoat Place
London SW1P 1PH
Tel: 020 7306 0606
Fax: 020 7306 0808
Helpline: 0845 300 0336 (Mon–Fri 8.30am–6.30pm)
Email: enquiries@alzheimers.org.uk
Website: www.alzheimers.org.uk

Information and helpline for carers of people with Alzheimer's disease. Has local support groups and funds research. Arranges training courses for carers and health professionals.

ARP Alcohol Recovery Project
2nd Floor, 7 Holyrood
London SE1 2EL
Tel: 020 7234 9940
Fax: 020 7357 6712
Email: info@arp-uk.org
Website: www.arp-uk.org

Provides housing, tenancy support, advice and face-to-face counselling within the London area for people with drink problems.

ASH (Action on Smoking and Health)
102–108 Clifton Street
London EC2A 4HW
Tel: 020 7739 5902
Fax: 020 7613 0531
Helpline: 0800 169 0169
Email: enquiries@ash.org.uk
Website: www.ash.org.uk

National organisation with local branches. Campaigns on anti-smoking policies. Offers free information on website or for sale from HQ. Catalogue on request.

Association for Post Natal Illness
145 Dawes Road
London SW6 7EB
Tel: 020 7386 0868 (Mon, Wed, Fri 10am–2pm; Tues, Thurs 10am–5pm)
Fax: 020 7386 8885
Email: info@apni.org
Website: www.apni.org

Offers help and advice for sufferers and families affected by postnatal illness. Network of local contacts.

Benefits Enquiry Line
Tel: 0800 882200 (8.30am–6.30pm weekdays)
Minicom: 0800 243355
Website: www.dwp.gov.uk
N. Ireland: 0800 220674

State benefits information line for sick or disabled people and their carers.

British Association for Counselling and Psychotherapy (BACP)
BACP House, 35–37 Albert Street
Rugby CV21 2SG
Tel: 0870 443 5252
Fax: 0870 443 5161
Helpline: 0870 443 5252
Minicom: 0870 443 5252
Email: bacp@bacp.co.uk
Website: www.bacp.co.uk

Professional services organisation and directory of professional counsellors. Offers lists of all levels of counsellors and can refer to local specialist counselling services.

Brook Centres
Studio 421, Highgate Studios
53–79 Highgate Road, London NW5 1TL
Tel: 020 7284 6040
Fax: 020 7284 6050
Helpline: 0800 018 5023

Email: admin@brookcentres.org.uk
Website: www.brook.org.uk

Offers free, confidential helpline to young people aged up to 25 years on contraception, sexual health and personal relationships. Recorded information also available on 020 7617 8000.

Carers UK
20–25 Glasshouse Yard
London EC1A 4JT
Tel: 020 7490 8818
Fax: 020 7490 8824
Helpline: 0808 808 7777
Email: info@carersuk.org
Website: www.carersuk.org

Offers information, support and advice on the practical, financial and emotional aspects of being a carer through a network of branches.

ChildLine
45 Folgate Street
London E1 6GL and
ChildLine FREEPOST NATN 1111
London E1 6BR
Tel: 020 7650 3200
Fax: 020 7650 3201
Helplines: 0800 1111 (24 hours a day, 365 days a year) and 0800 884444 (3.30–9.30pm weekdays; 2–8pm weekends)
Textphone: 0800 400222 (9.30am–9.30pm weekdays; weekends 9.30am–8pm)
Website: www.childline.org.uk

Confidential, free, counselling helpline for children and young people in trouble or danger 24 hours a day, every day. Comforts, advises and protects and, where a child is in danger, works with other helping agencies to ensure the child's protection. Free mobile networks include 3, BT mobile, Fresh, O2, Orange, T mobile, Virgin and Vodafone.

Compassionate Friends
53 North Street, Bedminster
Bristol BS3 1EN
Tel: 0845 120 3785
Fax: 0845 120 3786
Helpline: 0845 123 2304 (10am–4pm and 6.30–10.30pm 365 days/year)
Email: info@tcf.org.uk
Website: www.tcf.org.uk

Befrienders who offer information and support to parents, siblings and close family members who have lost a child. Support groups locally run by people who have themselves been bereaved.

Cruse Bereavement Care
Cruse House, 126 Sheen Road
Richmond TW9 1UR
Tel: 020 8939 9530
Fax: 020 8940 7638
Helpline: 0870 167 1677 (9.30am–5pm weekdays)
Bereavement line: 0845 758 5565
Young person's helpline: 0808 808 1677
Email: info@crusebereavementcare.org.uk
Website: www.crusebereavementcare.org.uk

Offers information and practical advice, sells literature, and has local branches that can provide one-to-one counselling to people who have been bereaved. Training in bereavement counselling for professionals.

Depression Alliance

212 Spitfire Studios, 63–71 Collier Street
London N1 9BE
Tel: 020 7833 2500
Fax: 020 7278 6747
Helpline: 0845 123 2320
Email: information@depressionalliance.org
Website: www.depressionalliance.org

Offers support and understanding to anyone affected by depression and for relatives who want help. Has a network of self-help groups, correspondence schemes and a range of literature; send SAE for information.

Eating Disorders Association

1st Floor, Wensum House, 103 Prince of Wales Road
Norwich NR1 1DW
Tel: 0870 770 3256
Fax: 01603 664915
Helpline: 0845 634 1414
Textphone: 01603 753322
Youth textphone 07977 493345
Email: info@edauk.com
Website: www.edauk.com

Offers information, help and support to anyone affected by eating disorders – anorexia and bulimia nervosa. Has a youthline (0845 634 7650) and local self-help groups.

Family Planning Association
2–12 Pentonville Road
London N1 9FP
Tel: 020 7837 5432
Fax: 020 7837 3042
Helpline: 0845 310 1334 (Mon–Fri 9am–6pm)
Website: www.fpa.org.uk

Offers telephone advice on contraception and sexual
health. Appointment needed to view their reference
library. Has a useful source of up-to-date information
about other services and organisations relating to
women's health.
Bangor: 01248 353534
Belfast: 028 9032 5488
Cardiff: 029 2064 4034
Derry: 028 7126 0016
Glasgow: 0141 576 5088

Fellowship of Depressives Anonymous
PO Box FDA
Self Help, Nottingham
Ormiston House, 32–36 Pelham Street
Nottingham NG1 2EG
Tel: 0870 774 4320
Fax: 0870 774 4319
Email: fdainfo@aol.com
Website: www.depressionanon.co.uk

Organisation run as a source of support for sufferers
from depression, complementary to professional care.
Membership offers newsletters, pen-friend and phone-
friend schemes.

Gamblers Anonymous
PO Box 88
London SW10 0EU
Tel: 020 7384 3040
Helpline: 0870 050 8880
Email: litrequest@gamblersanonymous.org.uk
Website: www.gamblersanonymous.org.uk

Offers face-to-face counselling and self-help recovery
programme to compulsive gamblers in group therapy
setting. Trains professionals.

GamCare
Units 2 and 3, Baden Place
Crosby Row, London SE1 1YW
Tel: 020 7378 5200
Fax: 020 7378 5237
Helpline: 0845 600 0133 (24 hours a day)
Email: info@gamcare.org.uk
Website: www.gamcare.org.uk

Offers help to anyone addicted to gambling.

Help the Aged
207–221 Pentonville Road
London N1 9UZ
Tel: 020 7278 1114
Fax: 020 7278 1116
Helpline: 0808 800 6565
Email: info@helptheaged.org.uk
Website: www.helptheaged.org.uk

Offers advice and a range of free information leaflets on benefits, community and residential care, and housing options.

Northern Ireland
Ascot House, Shaftesbury Square
Belfast BT2 7DB
Tel: 028 9023 0666
Fax: 028 9024 8183
Email: infoni@helptheaged.org.uk

Scotland
11 Granton Square
Edinburgh EH5 1HX
Tel: 0131 551 6331
Fax: 0131 551 5415
Email: infoscot@helptheaged.org.uk

Wales
12 Cathedral Road
Cardiff CF11 9LJ
Tel: 029 2034 6550
Fax: 029 2039 0898
Email: infocymru@helptheaged.org.uk

Manic Depression Fellowship
Castle Works, 21 St George's Road
London SE1 6ES
Tel: 0845 634 0540
Fax: 020 7793 2639
Email: mdf@mdf.org.uk
Website: www.mdf.org.uk

Offers support, via self-help groups, to enable people affected by manic depression (bipolar disorder) to take control of their lives. Has 24-hour legal advice line, travel insurance and life assurance schemes, self-management training and employment advice.

MIND (National Association for Mental Health)
Granta House, 15–19 Broadway
London E15 4BQ
Tel: 020 8519 2122
Fax: 020 8522 1725
Information line: 0845 766 0163
Email: contact@mind.org.uk
Website: www.mind.org.uk

Mental health organisation working for a better life for everyone experiencing mental distress. Has interpreting service for 100 languages. Offers support via local branches. Publications available on 0844 448 4448.

Miscarriage Association
c/o Clayton Hospital, Northgate
Wakefield, West Yorkshire WF1 3JS
Tel: 01924 200795 (Mon–Fri 9am–4pm)
Fax: 01924 298834
Helpline: 01924 200799 (Mon–Fri 9am–4pm)
Scottish helpline: 0131 334 8883
Email: info@miscarriageassociation.org.uk
Website: www.miscarriageassociation.org.uk

Offers information on miscarriage and ectopic pregnancy. Has UK-wide self-help support groups.

National Family Mediation
Devon & Exeter Institution
7 The Close
Exeter EX1 1EZ
Tel: 01392 668090
Fax: 01392 204227
Helpline: 0117 904 2825
Email: general@nfm.org.uk
Website: www.nfm.u-net.com

Umbrella for 60 non-profit family mediation services in
England and Wales offering help to couples, married or
unmarried, who are in the process of separation or divorce.

National Phobic Society
Zion Community Resource Centre
339 Stretford Road, Hulme, Manchester M15 4ZY
Tel/helpline: 0870 122 2325
Fax: 0161 227 9862
Email: nationalphobic@btconnect.com
Website: www.phobics-society.org.uk

Provides information, has support groups and can refer
to trained hypnotherapists, cognitive therapists and
other complementary therapists.

Nexus
6 The Quay
Bideford EX39 2HW
Tel: 01237 471704
Information line: 0800 834221
Website: www.nexus-uk.co.uk

An association of unattached people – not a helpline – looking to widen their social lives. People can be referred to groups in their areas.

NHS Direct (England, Northern Ireland and Wales)
Tel: 020 8867 1367 (admin)
Helpline: 0845 4647
Textphone: 0845 606 4647
Website: www.nhsdirect.nhs.uk
NHS Scotland 0800 224488

NHS Direct is a 24-hour helpline offering confidential health-care advice, information and referral service 365 days of the year. A good first port of call for any health advice.

National Institute for Health and Clinical Excellence (NICE)
MidCity Place, 71 High Holborn
London WC1V 6NA
Tel: 020 7067 5800
Fax: 020 7067 5801
Textphone: 0800 783 6783
Email: nice@nice.nhs.uk
Website: www.nice.org.uk

Provides guidance on the promotion of good health and the prevention and treatment of ill-health. Patient information leaflets are available for each piece of guidance issued.

Parentline Plus
520 Highgate Studios, 53–79 Highgate Road
Kentish Town, London NW5 1TL

Tel: 020 7284 5500
Fax: 020 7284 5501
Helpline: 0808 800 2222
Email: contact@parentlineplus.org.uk
Website: www.parentlineplus.org.uk

Provides general information on its confidential and
anonymous telephone helpline and runs parenting
courses. Accepts referral via Social Services.

Prodigy Website
Sowerby Centre for Health Informatics at Newcastle
(SCHIN), Bede House, All Saints Business Centre
Newcastle upon Tyne NE1 2ES
Tel: 0191 243 6100
Fax: 0191 243 6101
Email: prodigy-enquiries@schin.co.uk
Website: www.prodigy.nhs.uk/PILS/indexself.asp

A website mainly for GPs giving information for patients
listed by disease plus named self-help organisations.

Quit
211 Old Street
London EC1V 9NR
Tel: 020 7251 1551
Fax: 020 7251 1661
Helpline: 0800 002200
Scotland 0800 848484
Email: info@quit.org.uk
Website: www.quit.org.uk

Offers individual advice on giving up smoking,
including Asian languages, and talks to schools, and

can refer to local support groups. Offers training courses for health and education professionals.

QuitLines (for help in stopping smoking)
Helpline: 0800 169 0169
N. Ireland: 028 9049 2007

NHS helpline for those wanting help to stop smoking.

Relate (Marriage Guidance)
Herbert Gray College, Little Church Street
Rugby CV21 3AP
Tel: 01788 573241
Fax: 01788 535007
Helpline: 0845 130 4010
Email: enquiries@national.relate.org.uk
Website: www.relate.org.uk

Offers relationship counselling via local branches. Relate publications on health, sexual, self-esteem, depression, bereavement and re-marriage issues available from bookshops, libraries or via website.

Release (Drug-related problems)
388 Old Street, London EC1V 9LT
Tel: 020 7729 9904
Fax: 020 7729 2599
Helpline: 0845 450 0215 (Mon–Fri 10am–5.30pm)
Email: ask@release.org.uk
Website: www.release.org.uk

Offers information to users and their families and friends and a specialist heroin helpline for addicts and their families: 020 7749 4053.

National helpline ASK FRANK
Helpline: 0800 776600

Government helpline offering information and
literature and list of local clinics.

Samaritans
Head office: The Upper Mill, Kingston Road
Ewell, Surrey KT17 2AF
Tel: 020 8394 8300
Fax: 020 8394 8301
Helpline: 08457 909 090
Email: jo@samaritans.org
Website: www.samaritans.org

Offers confidential telephone support (24 hours a day,
365 days a year) to people who feel suicidal or
despairing and need someone to talk to. Local
branches listed in telephone directory; most also see
visitors at certain times of the day.

SANDS (Stillbirth and Neonatal Death Society)
28 Portland Place
London W1B 1LY
Tel: 020 7436 7940
Fax: 020 7436 3715
Helpline: 020 7436 5881 (10am–3pm Mon–Fri)
Email: support@uk-sands.org
Website: www.uk-sands.org

Offers information and support, via local self-help
groups and email, to parents and their families whose
baby has died before, during or shortly after birth. Also
offers support and training to health-care professionals.

Sexual Health and National AIDS Helpline
Helpline: 0800 567123

Free 24-hour government helpline giving confidential advice on HIV, AIDS and other sexually transmitted infections.

SureStart
Website: www.surestart.gov.uk

Provides information on health, social inclusion, grants and funding, local services and integration as well as child care and education.

Terrence Higgins Trust
52–54 Grays Inn Road
London WC1X 8JU
Tel: 020 7831 0330
Fax: 020 7242 0121
Helpline: 0845 122 1200 (10am–10pm Mon–Fri; 12 noon–6pm Sat and Sun)
Email: info@tht.org.uk
Website: www.tht.org.uk

Leading HIV charity offering information, advice and support to anyone who is at risk, living with or affected by HIV.

Victim Support
Cranmer House, 39 Brixton Road
London SW9 6DZ
Tel: 020 7735 9166
Fax: 020 7582 5712
Helpline: 0845 303 0900

Email: contact@victimsupport.org.uk
Website: www.victimsupport.org.uk

Refers people to local groups in the UK who offer emotional and practical support to victims of crime and those affected by crime.

Weight Concern
Brook House, 2–16 Torrington Place
London WC1E 7HN
Tel: 0207 679 6636
Fax: 020 7813 2848
Website: www.weightconcern.org.uk

A charity working to address both the physical and the psychological health needs of overweight people.

WorkSMART
Website: www.worksmart.org.uk

Provided by the TUC and includes information on employees' rights, money issues and your health at work, including stress.

WPF Counselling and Psychotherapy (previously Westminster Pastoral Foundation)
23 Kensington Square
London W8 5HN
Tel: 020 7361 4800
Fax: 020 7361 4808
Email: training@wpf.org.uk
Website: www.wpf.org.uk

Offers information, individual counselling and group

therapy at 29 UK centres on a sliding scale of fees. Has a wide range of training courses for professionals.

Yoga Therapy Centre
90–92 Pentonville Road
London N1 9HS
Tel: 020 7689 3040
Fax: 020 7689 3048
Email: enquiries@virgin.net
Website: www.yogatherapy.org

Offers information on yoga therapy to help people with a wide range of medical conditions. Also offers training in yoga therapy and carries out research.

The internet as a source of further information

After reading this book, you may feel that you would like further information on the subject. The internet is of course an excellent place to look and there are many websites with useful information about medical disorders, related charities and support groups.

It should always be remembered, however, that the internet is unregulated and anyone is free to set up a website and add information to it. Many websites offer impartial advice and information that have been compiled and checked by qualified medical professionals. Some, on the other hand, are run by commercial organisations with the purpose of promoting their own products. Others still are run by pressure groups, some of which will provide carefully assessed and accurate information whereas others may be suggesting medications or treatments that are not supported by the medical and scientific community.

Unless you know the address of the website you want to visit – for example, www.familydoctor.co.uk – you may find the following guidelines useful when searching the internet for information.

Search engines and other searchable sites

Google (www.google.co.uk) is the most popular search engine used in the UK, followed by Yahoo! (http://uk.yahoo.com) and MSN (www.msn.co.uk). Also popular are the search engines provided by Internet Service Providers such as Tiscali and other sites such as the BBC site (www.bbc.co.uk).

In addition to the search engines that index the whole web, there are also medical sites with search facilities, which act almost like mini-search engines, but cover only medical topics or even a particular area of medicine. Again, it is wise to look at who is responsible for compiling the information offered to ensure that it is impartial and medically accurate. The NHS Direct site (www.nhsdirect.nhs.uk) is an example of a searchable medical site.

Links to many British medical charities can be found at the Association of Medical Research Charities' website (www.amrc.org.uk) and at Charity Choice (www.charitychoice.co.uk).

Search phrases

Be specific when entering a search phrase. Searching for information on 'cancer' will return results for many different types of cancer as well as on cancer in general. You may even find sites offering astrological information. More useful results will be returned by using search phrases such as 'lung cancer' and 'treatments for lung cancer'. Both Google and Yahoo!

offer an advanced search option that includes the ability to search for the exact phrase; enclosing the search phrase in quotes, that is, 'treatments for lung cancer', will have the same effect. Limiting a search to an exact phrase reduces the number of results returned but it is best to refine a search to an exact match only if you are not getting useful results with a normal search. Adding 'UK' to your search term will bring up mainly British sites, so a good phrase might be 'lung cancer' UK (don't include UK within the quotes).

Always remember that the internet is international and unregulated. It holds a wealth of valuable information but individual sites may be biased, out of date or just plain wrong. Family Doctor Publications accepts no responsibility for the content of links published in this series.

Index

Your pages

We have included the following pages because they may help you manage your illness or condition and its treatment.

Before an appointment with a health professional, it can be useful to write down a short list of questions of things that you do not understand, so that you can make sure that you do not forget anything.

Some of the sections may not be relevant to your circumstances.

We are always pleased to receive constructive criticism or suggestions about how to improve the books. You can contact us at:

Email: familydoctor@btinternet.com
Letter: Family Doctor Publications
         PO Box 4664
         Poole
         BH15 1NN

Thank you

Health-care contact details

Name:

Job title:

Place of work:

Tel:

Name:

Job title:

Place of work:

Tel:

Name:

Job title:

Place of work:

Tel:

Name:

Job title:

Place of work:

Tel:

Significant past health events – illnesses/ operations/investigations/treatments

Event	Month	Year	Age (at time)

Appointments for health care

Name:

Place:

Date:

Time:

Tel:

Name:

Place:

Date:

Time:

Tel:

Name:

Place:

Date:

Time:

Tel:

Name:

Place:

Date:

Time:

Tel:

Appointments for health care

Name:

Place:

Date:

Time:

Tel:

Name:

Place:

Date:

Time:

Tel:

Name:

Place:

Date:

Time:

Tel:

Name:

Place:

Date:

Time:

Tel:

Current medication(s) prescribed by your doctor

Medicine name:

Purpose:

Frequency & dose:

Start date:

End date:

Medicine name:

Purpose:

Frequency & dose:

Start date:

End date:

Medicine name:

Purpose:

Frequency & dose:

Start date:

End date:

Medicine name:

Purpose:

Frequency & dose:

Start date:

End date:

Other medicines/supplements you are taking, not prescribed by your doctor

Medicine/treatment:

Purpose:

Frequency & dose:

Start date:

End date:

Medicine/treatment:

Purpose:

Frequency & dose:

Start date:

End date:

Medicine/treatment:

Purpose:

Frequency & dose:

Start date:

End date:

Medicine/treatment:

Purpose:

Frequency & dose:

Start date:

End date:

Questions to ask at appointments
(Note: do bear in mind that doctors work under great time
pressure, so long lists may not be helpful for either of you)

Questions to ask at appointments

(Note: do bear in mind that doctors work under great time pressure, so long lists may not be helpful for either of you)

Notes

Notes

Notes